CLOSE CALLS

CLOSE CALLS

The Confessions of a NFL Referee

NORM SCHACHTER

WILLIAM MORROW AND COMPANY, INC.

New York   *1981*

Library of Congress Cataloging in Publication Data

Schachter, Norm.
  Close calls.

  1. Schachter, Norm.   2. Football—Referees—
Biography.   3. National Football League.   I. Title.
GV939.S29A33   796.332′092′4   [B]   81—11341
ISBN 0-688-00794-5   AACR2

Printed in the United States of America

    2   3   4   5   6   7   8   9   10

BOOK DESIGN BY MICHAEL MAUCERI

Contents

CLOSE CALLS

Even Your Best
Friends Will Tell You

The gun went off. I ducked instinctively, and ran. Ran right toward the referee's dressing room. With the way the game had gone, I wasn't taking any chances. Especially with 60,000 fans roaring, "Kill that sonavabitch, kill that sonavabitch." When you're that sonavabitch they want to kill, it's time to run real fast. Anyplace.

As I ran, I couldn't help but think back to a game I had refereed in Wrigley Field. That's Coach George Halas' territory. Halas was on my back all afternoon. He kept screaming, "Norm, you're screwing me. Be consistent. Screw the Colts too."

Halas played no favorites. He kept after Stan Javie, the back judge. Javie has good judgment, is experienced and fearless. He has the guts to make the tough call against the home team with a few seconds left in a ball game. And he doesn't take himself too seriously. That's a successful official in the National Football League.

After a bitter growl from Coach Halas, I looked up at the stadium clock. It showed only a few seconds left in the game. I moved into a position where I could beat Halas down the sideline to the dressing room. I also spotted Javie walk behind Halas on the sideline, take out his gun and shoot it. Right behind Halas' back. That ended the game. Halas jumped 10 feet straight up into the air. I didn't wait to see him come down. I took off. As quick as I was, Javie was waiting in the dressing room. We both laughed. I didn't hear any laughter from behind the door. Halas kept pounding our

9

door. One good thing about working in this league: there's always a strong door on the referee's dressing room. There is also a game every week, so someone else has a turn.

But I wasn't laughing on the day the 60,000 fans wanted to kill that sonavabitch. I knew I needed help. Fortunately, I got it from a policeman assigned to the officials. He helped me fight my way clear of the crowd. The policeman steered me through a narrow opening and off the field. The fans were lined up at the exit of the field, yelling, screaming and pointing. They were wild. My last call had gone against the home team.

The policeman and I fought our way to the dressing room. We jumped inside, slammed the door shut and listened to the angry mob outside the closed door. I was damn glad for the policeman's help. I turned around to him and said, "Officer, I just want to thank you for your help. I do appreciate it. Thanks very much."

The policeman looked at me, growled and said, "Don't thank me. If I wasn't wearing this uniform, I'd kick your ass myself."

He would have too! Damned sorehead.

The gunshot didn't just end the ball game. It also was the end of 22 fun-filled, exciting years as a referee in the NFL. I had decided to hang it up. Before anyone else would ask me. I had been lucky. In fact, it's better to be lucky than good in our business. I had gotten more than my rightful share of gold rings on the 22-year ride on the football merry-go-round. It was time to put away my whistle. No, not where the coaches told me to put it. It also was time to shed those ridiculous white short pants and the striped shirt. It was all over, except for a post-season play-off game.

The entire weekend had helped make up my mind to call it a day. The plane had landed in Detroit around 5:30 P.M. The weather in Detroit was in the low twenties. It had been 82 degrees in Los Angeles when I left that Saturday morning. My top coat had been stolen before I even boarded the plane. Somebody was trying to tell me something. The plane felt its way into the Detroit airport. The weather was miserable. I said a silent prayer as the plane landed. I'm not the demonstrative type. The guy next to me was a bit more concerned. He was praying out loud. It had been a rough trip. If the game on Sunday would be anything like the plane ride, maybe I would quit a day earlier.

The weather was cold, extremely cold. The crew couldn't get

the automatic ramp out from the loading gate. The gears were frozen. They rolled out a movable ramp, attached it to the galley of the plane and opened the emergency door. I was first in line. I assumed that children and women were first only in lifeboats. I was first all right. First one to take a step. I hit some ice, and bounced down the stairs all the way on my ass and elbows. I was so damn embarrassed that I was grateful to the old lady who picked me up. I just got the hell out of there. That should have keyed me how the game would go the next day. It did too.

For 22 years I was the luckiest man in the world. I was a professional football referee. I got nothing but help, and from everybody. It's like I said. It's just a day late. It's the only job in the world where all kinds of people tell you what to do, how to do it, and then "How come you blew it?" I had to be perfect the first game of the season, and then get better every week as the season went on.

Everyone gets into the act. Even my eye doctor. You won't believe this, but it's true. All referees have their eyes examined annually. If you can't see, you don't work. That will startle some, I'm sure. Only my eye doctor knows and he won't tell.

I used to wear contact lenses. That's when I was worried about seeing the play. After a while, I took them out. But I was wearing the contact lenses that day in Wrigley Field for the championship game between the Chicago Bears and the New York Giants.

It was half time. The Giants and Bears were going at it. I was sitting in the dressing room, reviewing the first half with the other officials. We were getting geared up for the second half. There's no truth to the rumor that we officials decide at half time which team is going to win.

There was a knock at our dressing-room door. Someone yelled through the door, "Telegram for Referee Schachter."

I hurried to get it, wondering what it was all about. It was from my eye doctor in Los Angeles who had fitted me with my contact lenses. The telegram read, "SAW THE FIRST HALF. TIME FOR A NEW PRESCRIPTION."

Would you believe that clown added the price of the telegram to my next bill?

A week after my final game in Detroit, Art McNally, Supervisor of Officials, notified me that I was to referee Super Bowl X. It was the third time around for me. I had worked Super Bowl I in Los Angeles, Super V in Miami, and now it would be Super Bowl X in Miami again. Art didn't have to tell me, but he did.

"Norm, remember. Don't tell anyone you're going to be the referee. We'll release that information the Friday before the game."

I laughed to myself. You do that a lot when you're a football referee. The first time I had heard that was 22 years ago. Bert Bell, then Commissioner of the League, had called me. I wasn't in the office. The message I found on my desk was "Call Bert Bell at Pennypacker 5-7631."

Hell, someone was putting me on. I had been refereeing high school and college games for many years. Every referee hopes to work in the NFL. It is the big time. It had to be a gag from a friend or a bitter college coach. I never did return the call. Bert Bell called me a day later.

"Say, Norm. Aren't you interested in working in professional football? First thing you will have to learn is to return calls to Bert Bell."

It was for real. I apologized and made peace. I was hired over the phone. Bell then told me, "Norm, don't release the information of being hired by the NFL. We'll release it later on."

I don't know what later on is. I had been with the League 22 years. Worked over 400 professional football games, traveled over two and a half million miles by plane, worked three Super Bowl games, besides a half-dozen or so championship games, and the League still hasn't released that information. Television has taken care of it.

I went early to Miami for Super Bowl X. About a week or so before the game. I boarded the plane, took my customary seat, 3A, in first class. The League is a first-class operation. Our contract stipulates first class. It should be that way, for a referee needs his rest and comfort before the game. He certainly needs it after the game. During the game he is on his own and things often aren't as comfortable as Seat 3A. For years I thought the luggage was put in the back part of the plane behind the curtain. I learned that there were seats there when my wife flew with me. She sat up front in 3A, and I sat behind the curtain. And she doesn't even know a rule?

I opened my book. It isn't too smart to talk to strangers. We don't know who they are. Or what they will say we said. I learned my lesson my first year in the League. That year a man next to me found out that I was a referee in the NFL on my way to Green Bay. Laughingly, he asked, "Who's going to win?"

Without thinking, I popped off, "I don't know. I haven't read my script yet. I do that just before kickoff time."

I thought I was clever. Clever, hell. That guy gave me one of those side-angle looks that screams, "Ha! That's what I always thought. You referees decide the result and score of the game before the whistle even blows."

For years I went through a conversational routine on my trips back and forth across the country. The person sitting next to me on the plane looked at me, spotted my name tag on the back of my seat, and then said, "Excuse me, you look familiar. Are you anybody?"

I shook my head. "No, I'm nobody. Just another guy named Norm."

My seatmate nodded, then did a quick double-take. "I know who you are. You're Norm Schachter, the NFL referee. Aren't you?"

Before I could answer, I caught hell for all the bets he had lost over the years, the calls I had blown, and the lousy officiating he had seen on the tube. The final straw was his trying to find out the score of the next day's game.

I got smart the next time. I lied a wee bit. I never mentioned football. I said, "No. I'm a school administrator." That seemed safe enough.

That was the wrong thing to say or admit. I caught hell for that. I was blamed for the dope problem, low reading scores, disrespect for law and order, assaults on teachers, and the high cost of education.

No problem anymore. I finally found it. Now when we're flying 35,000 feet above the ground and the "Are you anybody?" routine starts, I lower my voice and whisper, "I'm an undertaker."

My seatmate becomes tongue-tied. Not another word is spoken. After a decent interval he gets up, changes his seat and keeps wondering if anything has rubbed off on him. The word spreads. Everyone steers clear of me. I'm left alone to concentrate on being an austere and deadly serious official. While doing so I find myself reviewing some wonderful memories of professional football over the past 22 years. Some good, some not so good. So many oddball bounces and so many controversial close calls have occurred that I realize I am fortunate to be alive. But the laughs and the excitement help compensate for the tensions of the job. Of course, there are not too many laughs during the ball game. That is a sure bet. I wouldn't laugh on the field during a game if my life depended upon it. Once I laughed during a time-out on the field. I was talking to Joe Connell, my umpire, and he told me something that had happened at home. It had nothing to do with football or the game, players or the coaches. Did I catch hell!

"What the hell's so funny? We're knocking our teeth out, runnin' our asses to the ground and you think it's funny," growled Sam Huff, the middle linebacker of the Giants.

Soon after the game we received verbal communication from the League office that officials were not to stand together. And—not to laugh on the field. Save the laughs for the ride home.

All the way to Miami I thought of how the game had changed and how the rules had been rewritten. Referees had become more professional. Their pay had gone up along with that of the players. The players were bigger, faster, quicker and (I believe) tougher. So many coaches had come and gone. Some were fun to work and others weren't. A few coaches were so much better in preparation, game plan and organization. They would win more than their rightful share of ball games. Reporters were more knowledgeable, more demanding for right answers and more critical. Television commentators were sharper. Many of them had been former players and had gone through the battles on the field. And instant replay was face-to-face with the referees—and I never did take a good picture.

If you believe it is easy for me to forget the responsibilities of all those "fun-filled" years, consider what happened after a Steeler-Oilers game a couple of seasons ago.

The game had ended with a controversy. Pittsburgh had just recovered their onside kick after it had gone the necessary 10 yards. Unfortunately, the official closest to the play ruled that the ball had been touched before it had gone the 10 yards. The Steelers had to rekick with a five-yard penalty. Houston received the kickoff and ran out the clock to win the game.

As I left the press box, where I was observing the officials for the League office, I ran across someone from the Pittsburgh organization whom I had known for many, many years. He looked at me. "Well, you blew that one, Norm."

"Wait a minute. I was up here in the press box, sitting close to you. I wasn't refereeing. I'm upstairs now."

He kept walking toward the elevator, shaking his head and muttering, "You blew it." It made me realize that once a referee always a referee. Players, coaches, writers and fans still think of me as a referee. Though this book was written when I was actively refereeing, I still think of it in the present. Don't be alarmed if it says that I am still refereeing, for I'm still actively involved with the officials, the rule book, the officials' exams, and editing the rule book. I observe the officials each week somewhere in the country—usually the nationally televised game.

On the way home from Houston the next morning, the man sitting next to me on the plane was reading the sports section. He looked at the controversial picture, looked over at me and asked, "Were you Norm Schachter?"

I still am. That's the way it is for a referee—always a referee.

You're Only as Good as Your Last Call

I remember my first penalty call as an NFL referee. It seems as if it just happened last Sunday, and I know it was at least 1,000 Sundays ago. And 1,000 penalty calls back. I can still see the white flag (now it's yellow) float through the air.

It was on a forward pass play in Los Angeles Memorial Coliseum. Norm Van Brocklin dropped back to pass. Come to think of it, Van Brocklin always dropped back to pass. He wouldn't run with the ball if his life depended upon it. Once, just once, Van Brocklin forgot himself and took off as he was chased. He realized that he was running with the ball, so he dropped to the ground, turned to me and said, "I must have lost my head."

This time "The Dutchman" dropped back into the pocket and looked downfield. The Pittsburgh defensive man, #44, pushed Elroy Hirsch in the end zone. That's defensive pass interference. I thought it was an easy call. Defensive pass interference in the end zone is not a score. But pretty close to it. The ball is placed on the one-yard line. That's the rule. Anyway, I put the ball on the one-yard line and signaled first down for the Rams. That's a helluva good field position. It's not a call to guess on. It has to be there, for it is almost a sure touchdown in a play or two. Almost certain in four downs.

I thought it was a great call. Number 44 didn't agree with me. He yelled at me, "I didn't touch him."

Nobody fouls in this league, especially those who do the fouling. At least that's what they tell me. It's always a bang-bang play. It's always the other guy. But that's why they pay the officials. Anyway, #44 yelled.

"That was a horseshit call. You've got your eyes up your ass," he screamed. Loud too.

It was all so new and different that I must have blinked. At least I felt a twinge in my ass. Maybe #44 was right about where my eyes were. Now, if any player swears at me, it is an automatic 15-yard penalty. That's unsportsmanlike conduct, especially if someone else can hear it.

Not then, though. I was so new, so wide-eyed. Nobody had ever sworn at me in the college games that I had officiated before I joined the pros. It bothered me, so I walked over to Norm Duncan, the back judge on the crew. He was an experienced old-timer and a damn good official.

"Hey, Duncan, how about that swearing. Do I have to take that shit? Or do I ignore it? What should I do?"

"Hell, forget it," said Duncan. "Don't pay any attention to it. They don't mean anything. It's just like saying, 'Have a nice day.'"

The game went on and within five minutes I saw Duncan's penalty flag fall to the ground. He had a foul on the Steelers, and it was on #44 for illegal use of the hands. Duncan explained the foul to #44 and then I saw him throw his flag a mile high into the air. When it came down, he measured off another 15 yards. It was for unsportsmanlike conduct.

When things quieted down, I eased over to Duncan and asked, "What was the unsportsmanlike conduct foul for, Dunc?"

Duncan looked at me and said, "Number Forty-four called me a no-good fuckin' bastard."

I must have done a double take. Duncan kept looking at me. "What's the matter, Norm?"

"Hell, Duncan, you just told me five minutes ago not to pay any attention to the swearing. You said that it didn't mean anything. That it was the same thing as saying, 'Have a nice day.'"

Duncan got that old-timers look on his face, and answered as he walked away, "This is different. This is personal."

That was the first lesson I learned as a referee in the National Football League. If it is personal, throw your flag. If it's just conversation, walk away and allow them to let off steam. Experience does pay off. Do I remember that first call? I sure do.

❋   ❋   ❋

It's a funny thing how one remembrance brings back other memories. I'm thinking back to a game more than twenty years ago. My oldest son, Tom, was about nine years old. Tom had gone to every game that I had worked in Los Angeles. It was easy, for I just took the family with me when I had a game in Los Angeles. That's home country. It's where I live. That Rams-49er game is another game that sticks in my mind. More from what Tom said to me after the game than the game itself.

It was a big game. Hell, they are all big games. This time I mean a big crowd. Probably the largest crowd ever to have watched a professional football game. It was a natural. Bitter rivals. Great players on both teams. The San Francisco 49ers and the Los Angeles Rams in the Los Angeles Coliseum. That's a nice package. I even remember the date. It was November 1, 1957. There were 102,368 fans in the stands. And that included my three sons and wife. I figured that at least those four were on my side. I wouldn't bet on the other 102,364 fans.

San Francisco had Hugh McElhenny, Y. A. Tittle and the "Alley Oop" pass catcher, R. C. Owens. The Rams had Van Brocklin, Elroy Hirsch, Jon Arnett, Tom Fears and Les Richter. They traded 11 men to get Richter and he was worth it. He was tough. The Rams won 37–24. Everyone had a great afternoon, but me. It seemed as if everything that I called, or didn't call, was worth yelling about. At least from the partisan fans. The boos were loud, noisy and pointed. Pointed right at me. It was a long afternoon, and a noisy one.

I couldn't help but wonder how my family was taking all the flack and comments made against me. They had good seats to listen to the wolves howling for my scalp. And they were howling. If you never pulled on a striped shirt, walked across the white lines of a professional football field, you can't help but wonder how it feels to have thousands and thousands of people scream and yell at you.

I couldn't tell how my loved ones were holding up against the bitterness toward me. There's no way of knowing how my family really feels when 50,000 to 100,000 people jump to their feet and let go with loud boos. Like yelling, "You blind asshole." That's not mentioning the millions of boos they can't hear from the people watching the game on television. The remarks are never complimentary. They are vicious. I keep telling myself that it's nothing personal. Like hell it isn't. I could kid myself, but could my family do that?

This particular Ram-49er game in the Coliseum was wild. A tough call went against the Rams. I made the call. The stands exploded! The people screamed, yelled and booed. I had to stop the game for four minutes. The quarterback couldn't make himself heard. No one could hear the signals. The game finally continued.

I waited patiently in the referee's dressing room until the crowd had thinned out. On the way home I carefully went over my prepared speech on how crowds treat officials, how impersonal it was though it sure sounded personal, and how partial hometown fans were.

I broke it down in very simple language. Nothing fancy. Just "It's nothing personal. I want you to know it's not me they're after. It's just the job and whoever is working the game, the fans will get after."

Finally after my little speech to my three sons, I turned to the oldest one and said, "Well, Tom, it didn't bother you any, now did it? You know what I am trying to say."

Tom looked me right in the eye. All nine years of him. "Yeah, I know what you are trying to say. And it is personal. I was booing louder than all of them. You booted that call."

This "personal" business sometimes has its lighter moments. If you stay on your toes and look for the oddball happenings. When Van Brocklin was coach of Minnesota, he had a middle linebacker, #58, who occasionally got careless and clotheslined an offensive end going out for a forward pass. "Clotheslining" is another word for holding out your arm straight from the side and bringing it across the opposing receiver's Adam's apple right under his chin as he runs by you. Unsuspectingly, of course. That smarts a bit. It usually makes the offensive receiver a bit cautious. He looks around, and sometimes forgets his pass patterns.

On the second play of a nationally televised game, #58 did his work on an unsuspecting receiver. Joe Connell, my umpire, only saw the tail end of the play which resulted in the receiver flipping on his back. Connell missed the clothesline as he was watching another player, but he knew what had happened. A good official doesn't call a foul unless he sees the entire action. We just don't guess. At least not as much as people think. All Connell saw was the end result. He knew he had been had, as was the end who was on the ground, flat on his back.

Connell and #58 had a few choice words. I walked over and said, "Joe, don't talk. Throw your flag if you see it."

No sooner had I said that when #58 turned to me and told me, "It's none of your business. Stay out of it."

I looked at #58. Maybe he thought I was an end who would go out for a pass. No way. I told him, "It is my business. Knock it off. Play ball."

As I turned to walk away, #58 yelled at me, "Mind your own business, you sonavabitch."

My flag was down. As I was walking off the 15 yards for un-sportsmanlike conduct (swearing at a referee) against #58 for his smart-ass remark, he walked with me and kept asking, "What's the penalty for, sir?"

I didn't answer. However, at the two-minute warning when I went to give Coach Van Brocklin the time, he was waiting for me.

"Say, Norm, what was the fifteen-yard penalty for?"

I knew I'd hear something. "Coach, Number Fifty-eight called me a sonavabitch and no one in this league, and I mean no one but you, can call me a sonavabitch without getting a penalty."

Van Brocklin looked at me, didn't smile, and said, "You sonava-bitch."

Halas and
That Fair Advantage

What in hell do coaches mean when they tell me, "I don't want any breaks. Just give me my fair advantage"? You would think someone would come up with an answer to that. The comments of the coaches and the players are geared toward getting that fair advantage. That's what makes the referee's job so much fun.

Since I started working as an NFL referee, I suppose more than one hundred head coaches have changed jobs. If I could count the assistants, it would probably total over 500. Of course, the head coaches get most of the criticism or the praise in the press or on television, and the coaches most people want to know more about are Vince Lombardi, Tom Landry, Don Shula, John Madden, Paul Brown and the one and only George Halas, who started the whole damn thing. Not necessarily in that order. All of them are and were dynamic coaches, expressive (some profane and some profound), well organized, and they knew how to relate to their personnel. All of them have been consistent winners. They looked for that fair advantage, worked to get it, and let you know immediately if the other team got it. I liked them all. The funny thing is that all of them, except Tom Landry, worked the referee all the time. Each had his own technique, each one was fair, consistent and hard-nosed in his own way. Landry is the quietest. Never complains and never changes expression. Takes the good bounces the same way he takes the bad bounces. The good breaks with the bad breaks.

All of them knew the rules, and more importantly, knew football. They were winners. No flash in the pan. Consistent winners year in and year out. As we say, we can't judge a player or coach by a one-year record. There have to be quite a number of years down the drain before a coach or player can be evaluated. I got a lot of laughs from them all. They may not have realized it, but I did. Not too many from Coach Landry, but I never got too much heat from him either. A true gentleman. The five others—Halas, Lombardi, Madden, Brown and Shula—were hecklers, needlers in their own way and winners. They would needle, but when the game was over, that was it. Nothing to the League office, no second-guessing (at least not too much) and everything started fresh the following week. Some other coaches never forget. They bring up incidents that happened a year ago, two years ago and even five years ago. That is, if they are still around.

Football coaches today are a different breed of cat. They growl differently too. At least from when I started in 1954. Football squads carry more players now. When I started to referee, the squads had 33 men. Now it's a 45-man squad. Coaching staffs are larger now too. Now a head coach carries eight to ten assistant coaches. And they are all specialists. The game is now more highly specialized. Each player position has its own coach. Coaches are not necessarily better than the ones in the fifties or sixties. Though I think they are. There is now so much for the head coach to do. It just isn't the new terminology that's changed. I'm not talking about new formations, different position names, or the specialized units. Players are faster, smarter, quicker, heavier, taller and more highly paid. When many players on a team make more money than the boss (coach), you have a built-in problem. Players are unionized and organized. They have their lawyers, tax accountants, investments, TV programs, commercials and shop foremen (players' representatives). The players are more recognizable because of the television exposure. Games are now played on Sunday, Monday, Thursday and Saturday.

A head coach today is an administrator, a personnel manager, a father confessor and a mother substitute. He is more knowledgeable. More professional. Coaches seldom swear nowadays. We have a few coaches in the League who still let loose a barrage of barroom language. You can count that number on the fingers of your left hand, if you lost two fingers of that hand in an electric saw accident. Players don't use coarse language today as they did when I first started to referee. It's a more highly specialized game today. That's also true of the officials on the field. These men are more professional, better screened and trained, more highly supervised and more qualified. Though the game is different today, it still comes down to blocking, tackling, running, throwing and kicking. Same basic things as years ago.

All NFL coaches are good. They have to be or they wouldn't be in their jobs. Everyone can't win. Even a good one will lose with poor material. But over the years the great coaches evaluate better, get players to perform better and try to get that fair advantage. The six coaches that I have mentioned are the best in my opinion. There have also been others who are top-notch and who have been consistent winners. Men like Sid Gillman, Chuck Noll, Weeb Ewbank, Hank Stram, George Allen and Bud Grant have proven themselves. How John Brodie rated me as a referee could well illustrate what I mean about different coaches and their abilities.

John Brodie is now an NBC color man for the National Football League games. He is good too. I knew he would be. He was an outstanding quarterback with San Francisco, a gentleman and a fellow with a helluva sense of humor. And he still doesn't take himself too seriously, though he takes his job seriously.

The 49ers were playing the Rams in San Francisco one Sunday afternoon a couple of seasons ago. Brodie thought he was roughed by Deacon Jones after he had thrown a forward pass. I didn't think so. That meant he wasn't roughed. Brodie charged me, waving his arms, pointing, screaming and acting very unBrodie-like. I walked away. That normally ended most discussions.

Not this time though. Brodie followed me. He kept up his noisy monologue. Finally, I had enough. I decided to get into the act.

"John, knock it off. I heard you say the same thing twelve times. You weren't roughed. Jones couldn't avoid you. Damn it, even you can't change direction in midair. He banged into you, but it wasn't roughness. Enough is enough. Let's play ball."

Brodie looked at me, saw that I was annoyed and said, "No hard feelings, Norm. I still think you're the second-best referee in the National Football League."

Second-best! Who the hell did he think was better? I also had my ego. Not too big a one, but I had one. It bugged me, but I blew my whistle to continue the game. The game ended on a peaceful note. The 49ers won. Brodie and I ran off the field together. I had maneuvered that. As I ran beside him, I asked, "Brodie, you said that I was the second-best referee in the NFL. Right?"

"That's right, you are. No one can argue that."

"Well, who do you think is the best?"

"All the other referees are tied for first."

All coaches have to be extra special to work in the NFL. When it comes to looking for that fair advantage, George Halas was thinking three plays ahead. Not only what play should be called, but what he would call the referee. Fortunately, he played no favorites. Whoever was working got it. Really got it. One thing though. If he was able "to run you," I mean get a fair advantage that wasn't there, he would run you right out of the League. Halas knew that any referee who could be intimidated by him would also be intimidated by another coach. That might cost him an important game sometime. George Halas started coaching the Bears in 1920. Nineteen twenty! That's over 60 years ago. We still think of him as the Chicago Bears. And he stopped coaching in 1967. What an impact he made! During his tenure as coach (and owner) he would fire himself for a year or so, and then would hire himself back. Halas respected guts, though he wanted it his way. He raised hell, stormed the sidelines and kept waving his program.

I remember once in Chicago when the Bears were playing the Detroit Lions. They both hit hard. Both these teams are in the black-and-blue division. Both play tough. No holds barred. Both teams looked for that fair advantage. When one of my calls went against the Bears, Halas shouted, swore and screamed. The language was a bit coarse and heavy. I walked over to the sideline just after I heard, "You blind sonavabitch." I didn't mind his language as long as it wasn't personal. The "you" made it sound personal.

I looked at Halas and said, "What did you say? Were you talking to me?"

Halas stared at me. He then looked down and stared at the football, which was lying close to the sideline. "I wasn't talking to you. I was talking to that damn ball. That no good lousy sonavabitch of a ball. It hasn't bounced right all afternoon. You shittin' ball."

Cursing the ball? He knew and I knew. It saved him 15 yards.

One Halas memory brings back many more. I'm thinking back to the championship game in Chicago when they beat the New York Giants by a score of 14–10. Halas always carried a folded program in his hand. Many coaches do. They keep looking at who's in the game. Not for their own players. They know them. But for the opponent's players.

Halas was in a league by himself when it came to the program in his hand. He used it as a weapon. Not to stick in the referee's eye. Just as a "waver." He would hold the program above his head or in front of him and let it move around. It was more expressive than words. Especially to excite the crowd.

George Halas was one of the founders of the National Football League, and also the owner of the ball club. He was in a league by himself when it came to whipping up a crowd and getting them mad. Not at himself, but at the referee. Like the time he did it to me in Chicago the day the Bears won the championship. They haven't won one since.

The weather was pushing zero, the players were pushing one another, and the coaches were pushing for that fair advantage. At the end of the first half it was still anybody's ball game. The partisan crowd in Chicago was screaming.

Millions of television fans must have dropped their cups and sat up in their chairs when they saw Coach Halas run up to me before the start of the second half. He ran all the way from his sideline out to the middle of the field where I was standing. He waved his program at me as he ran toward me. He waved his program close to my face, his mouth open and his jaws moving. Every word he said was punctuated with a wave of his program close to my face. The home crowd kept shouting, "You tell him, George. Attaboy, George."

Coach Halas wasn't telling, he was asking as he waved that damn program in his hand. He calmly asked in his own Halasese manner, "Which way are we going this half, Norm?"

When I pointed in the direction the Bears were to go, he thanked me by waving his program to my face. "Thanks, Norm." He started to move away. However, after he ran a few paces, he turned around and ran back to me. He wriggled his program at me for the last time and said, "Thanks again, Norm. Appreciate it."

Nothing I did was right after that as far as the crowd was concerned. I was lucky to get out of there alive. Maybe I wouldn't have if the Giants had won that day.

Coach Halas never stopped working the officials. He was the best at it. He did a con job that was a masterpiece. I enjoyed it. He tried all the time. Especially before the game, when things were quiet and he could talk to me. Halas was interested in consistency. They all are. If a referee is inconsistently bad, he's gone. That's the way it should be.

It was a crucial and critical game in Baltimore. The Bears and Colts were at it. It meant the division championship. Bert Bell was Commissioner then. He made the game assignments for the officials. When I walked out onto the field that Sunday afternoon in Baltimore, Halas was waiting for me. He started the con.

"Norm, I knew you were going to work this game. I called Bert Bell during the week and asked him who was going to work the game. He wouldn't mention any names. He did tell me that he was sending the best crew. I knew then you would be here. We look forward to your working the game. You've got great judgment. You don't call those chicken-shit fouls. Sure glad you are here for this game."

The game started. Within the first minute of play, I had to call a foul against the Bears. I heard from Halas. "Norm, that chicken-shit call of yours stinks. You stink. No goddamn judgment at all. Why the hell they had to bring you all the way back here from the West Coast kills me. We've got guys like you with your piss-poor judgment back here by the thousands. They are a dime a dozen. You no-good blind bastard."

I listened, laughed to myself and yelled over to him, "Hey, Coach. I'm the same guy you spoke to a few minutes ago. Don't you remember? Remember how pleased you were that I was here?"

Halas yelled back, "Bullshit. You're no shittin' good. I've always said that. I had you confused with someone else."

The players laughed. It could have been true. Not really. He knew every referee in the League. And those who were gone. Knew whom he could yell at, knew when to stop, and knew when to needle. He had that long sharp verbal needle going all the time. I liked it. Prior to other games which needed an extra bit of conning, Halas always meet me out on the field when I went looking for the captains. He always held a paper in his left hand. He had a pencil in his right hand.

"Say, Number Fifty-six, what's your name?"

He knew my name. He knew everybody's name. I didn't let on. I said, "Coach, my name is Smith. I'll spell it for you. S-M-I-T-H. Smith."

He wrote down Schachter. He was a favorite, but got no favors from me or any other crew that worked his games. That's the truth.

Coach Halas worked us all. At least he was consistent. Biff Gardner, now a retired umpire, always had a twinkle in his eye. When we worked together, we always managed to have a few laughs. Even if we had to pretend on a bad day.

Coach Halas jumped all over Gardner one day in Chicago. On a play near the sideline, Gardner called a clip on a Bear player. With that Halas exploded, or pretended to. You never really knew.

"Gardner, you dumpy clown. Go back to San Diego where you belong. If that was a clip, I'll kiss your ass in Marshall Field's window at high noon. Baa—baa—aaah."

Gardner slowly turned around, looked carefully at Halas and then calmly said, "George, do you think it will draw a crowd?"

The Bear players laughed. Not long though. Or loud. I wonder what Halas meant by "Baa—baa—aaah." I had never heard that one before.

Ed Marion worked as the head linesman on our crew for a number of years. He especially enjoyed the exchanges with George Halas. He got into it with Coach Halas pretty good one afternoon. It was another nationally televised game and a laugher. Not much of a game. Lots of talk, though, between Halas and Marion. That was par for the course.

I was standing in my referee's position in the middle of the field when I heard Halas go after Marion, who was on the Bears' side of the field.

"Hey, Marion, why don't you quit? You're an adult. Quit when you are ahead."

"I like it , George. I like the game and the company. I like you. Why should I quit?"

"Marion, you're fat. Why don't you quit?" Halas kept shouting. Just as loud, Marion yelled back, "I'm not fat."

For some reason Phil Handler, one of the Bears' assistant coaches, got into the act. "You're fat, Marion."

Marion didn't mind Halas. But Handler was a different act. Ed Marion turned around. "Handler, I'm not as fat as you are. I'll race you."

Before Handler could answer, Halas said, "Don't race him, Phil. What if he beats you?"

I looked over, laughed and thought, And all this on national television. I hope nobody hears any of this. Millions of people think everyone talks strategy. Maybe it was.

Another time we had a pre-season game in one of the smaller Southern cities. The sidelines were crowded. The security on the field was a little looser than the normal NFL field. They weren't used to the operation of a National Football League game. Ed Marion looked around in the second quarter after a loud blast from Halas. There was an older man wearing a security badge, trying to keep fans from wandering too close to the Chicago bench. Marion spotted Halas down his sideline, about the 25-yard line. Marion walked over to the old security guard, who was a lot older than Halas. Or so it seemed.

"Listen. Do you see that old man on the sideline with a program in his hand? The one with the hat and overcoat on. He isn't wearing any field pass. He shouldn't be there. He might get hurt. Why don't you get his ass out of there? If he gets hurt, you'll have a lawsuit, sure as hell. Do your job and get that old man out of there. Before he hurts himself. Besides, he's making a fool of himself yelling at the players and officials."

Marion had spoken to the old security man in a serious manner. The old fellow took it personally. He ran up to Halas, who was wearing the hat and overcoat without a field pass on, grabbed his arm and tried to run him off the field. Picture that if you can. There they were. Two older men, yelling, pushing and swearing. It was finally worked out. It was worth a laugh. Thanks, Marion.

* * *

The Bears were in Green Bay one Sunday, and it was another big game. They always are. That Sunday morning after the service, the officials were standing on the church steps, waiting for their ride. Coach Halas walked over. He never missed a Sunday. Ed Marion and he had just gone to communion together.

Halas walked up to Marion. "Marion, you can't screw us today. Remember you went to communion with me."

During the game, Marion called a 60-yard touchdown back as a Chicago tackle held on the play. Halas ran down the sideline the 60 yards, screaming and swearing at Marion.

Marion waited until Halas reached him, turned to him an innocently said, "George, how can you say things like that? I went to church with you today."

Halas yelled at him, "You're still a blind sonavabitch."

Something was bugging the defensive unit of the Chicago Bears one day in Wrigley Field. They were mad at something. But they were always mad at something.

This particular Sunday a defensive player jumped off sides. Ed Marion, the no-nonsense head linesman, threw his flag for offside. Then he threw it on the next play again for another offside. He threw his flag on four consecutive plays. The same penalty. All against the Bears.

After the fourth offside penalty, I walked over to Marion. "Ed, enough is enough. The next time you throw your flag for offside, I'll shove it up your ass."

"Like hell you will. Halas is testing me. He's always testing me."

"Ed, you passed the test. Let's play ball and get the game over. And get the hell out of here."

Marion passed the test. The defensive line got the word. They stayed on sides the rest of the game. Not Halas though. He was all over the sideline. Yelling at Marion. At half time he stopped Marion and me as we were walking off the field. He had his little piece of paper out in his hand. He shoved it under Marion's nose and said, "Look at this, Marion. You have eight fouls against the Bears and none against the Cardinals. Is that right?"

Marion stopped and looked at the paper. He handed it back to Halas and started to walk away. He said, "Coach, if that's what you say. I believe it. I know you wouldn't lie. It must be right. Eight against the Bears and none against the Cardinals. I take your word for it, George."

Dan Tehan worked with me as the head linesman of the crew before Marion joined us. Tehan worked as an official in the League for 33 years. He was the sheriff of Cincinnati so nothing surprised him. Whenever we went into Chicago to work for the Bears, he told me the same story about something that had happened long before Tehan joined the crew.

Tehan worked a long time so he had lots of stories. And he worked the Bears probably more times than anyone else in the League. I once accused him of receiving a varsity letter and a blanket from the Bears.

Tehan said, "We were in Chicago. It was fourth down with lots of yardage to go. It was deep in the Bears' territory so they had to kick. The punter was standing on his five-yard line when the center snapped the ball. It was a poor snap and went toward the kicker's right. The blocker on the right side of the kicker was a rookie. For some reason this rookie moved toward his left. When the punter kicked the ball, this rookie was right in front of him. The kick smacked the rookie right in the ass, and the ball rolled over the end line for a safety. I felt sorry for the rookie. I thought he would catch hell from Halas.

"Nothing like that at all. The rookie ran off the field, rubbing his ass as it was still smarting from the kick. Halas put his arm around the rookie's shoulders and asked him, 'Son, how do you feel?'

"The rookie, still rubbing his rear end, was surprised. He thought he was going to be chewed out by the master himself. He looked relieved when he answered as he rubbed, 'Fine, Coach, thanks. Why do you ask?'

"Halas looked him over and said, 'I thought for a minute you had a brain concussion.' "

Coach George Halas has a special spot in my memories. He was a fighter, utterly fearless. Wherever the Chicago Bears went to play, he managed to get the hometown fans wild. They would rant, rave and go off their rockers screaming at him. He played the part: scowling, gesturing and running all over the sidelines. It had to upset the other team. I just stood out on the field and en-joyed it. I kept thinking back to the first year I worked in the League. I was a field judge then. One of my responsibilities was to give the visiting team's head coach the five-minute warning be-fore the end of the half-time intermission. The five-minute warn-ing had to be given to the head coach personally. Just to the head coach and only to him. Not an assistant coach or to anyone else. Reason for that is that it gives the team time to wind up its half-time instructions. It also gives the head coach the responsibility to get his team out on the field in time for the second-half kickoff. If the field judge doesn't tell the head coach personally, the coach might say he never got the five-minute warning. It's a rule, and it's in the book. It's a part of the field judge's mechanics.

Emil "Dutch" Heintz was my referee that first year. He told me that Halas had a habit of not being available when the field judge went into the Bears' dressing room at half time to give the five-minute warning.

"Be sure to give the five-minute warning to Halas personally. Just to him. Not to anyone else. Look for him. Find him. Be sure to give it to him. Or he'll give it to you later" was Heintz's advice.

Heintz had been around a long, long time. He knew Halas well. I got to know Halas well very quickly. At half time I went into the Bears' dressing room. I looked for Coach Halas to give him the five-minute warning. I couldn't find him. Fortunately, I had gone into their dressing room seven minutes before the half time ended. I had a couple of minutes to find him.

One of his assistant coaches (I was so new I didn't even know his name) asked me, "What do you want?"

"Where's Coach Halas? I want to give him the five-minute warning."

"That's all right. I'll tell him."

"Oh, no. I have to give it to him personally. Where is he?"

"He's around here somewhere," he told me as he gave a fast turn and look.

I looked everywhere. Finally, I went into the toilet area. There he was, standing up in front of the urinal and pissing. Quite a touching moment for a rookie official.

I walked up to him, stood at his side and said, "Coach Halas, five-minute warning."

Halas kept pissing. Halas didn't turn his head. He just kept pissing. Time was getting short. So was I. Here I was. An adult. An official in the National Football League. Making my mark. And watching an older man pissing and not turning his head. Maybe if he turned suddenly, he would have pissed all over me.

Halas kept staring at the wall and looking straight ahead. I reached around and put up my five fingers in front of his face. "Five minutes, Coach." I took my hand down real fast. I'm sure he would have pissed all over it.

Finally, he said, "Okay. Five minutes. You've screwed me all first half, now you want to screw me on the time. Be sure you don't screw me in the second half."

I got out of there real fast.

When I worked the Bears and Halas, I never fell asleep out on the field. He kept me on my toes all those many years. Halas never let me take myself too seriously for he knew how to prick the bubble. How could I? All I had to do was to think back to the touching vignette of Halas and me in the pissery. George Halas was one of the all-time bests in this business. He helped make officials out of a lot of us. Especially me.

Vince Lombardi

Unless you have been chewed out by Lombardi, you haven't really been chewed out. It's been years since the last blast. He was really something. Tough and fair. He looked for his fair advantage. Screamed, hollered and ranted. An honest person, dedicated to winning the big ones. And the little ones. He did too. It seemed as if for every important game, every strange oddball bouncing game that Green Bay was involved in during their heyday, I was the referee. There was Super Bowl One, the Freeze Bowl against Dallas with the temperature below 30 degrees, and the Packers and Colts game that went into sudden death. That one put the extended goalpost in all ball parks after that game. And so many other games. I still can see Coach Vince Lombardi standing in front of his bench with his eyes ablaze and his mouth wide open. Or was it his eyes wide open and his mouth ablaze? Chewing at me if he thought I was wrong. But only if he thought I was wrong. He didn't spend time spinning his wheels, like some of them.

Lombardi was a winner. A gentleman. He never swore at an official. At least I never had heard him. He wouldn't refuse any breaks that came his way. A referee knew where he stood with Lombardi. He insisted on consistency. "Be consistent." If I heard him say it once, I heard him say it a dozen times. Now that I think of it, he always said it after a tough call I made that went against the Packers.

One game that still gives me chills was the Freeze Bowl. That's how the TV announcers called it. That's how sports writers labeled it. It was cold. Bitter cold. At least for a referee from southern California. I still get the shakes when I think of it. And I'm not a drinking man. That was the championship game between Green Bay and Dallas.

I had left for Green Bay from Los Angeles with the temperature in the mid-seventies. When I reached Chicago two days before the game, I knew immediately there was a problem. My connecting flight to Green Bay was weathered in. Later in the afternoon I caught a North Central flight to Green Bay. It was dark, cold, and snow flurries were flying all over. The plane landed in Green Bay. At least I think it was Green Bay. I couldn't see a thing. I rushed to get off. It was 10 degrees below zero. I got my bag, grabbed a cab and checked into the Northland Hotel. They had heat. A couple of us took a short, short walk after dinner. That should show you how stupid officials are. People in the streets (and they were there) looked at me and said, "Hey, Ref, don't catch cold. Keep warm. Keep those arms limbered up so you can signal Green Bay touchdowns." I am always amazed that people spot us. Maybe in Green Bay they can spot any stranger.

All day Saturday we reviewed our mechanics for the game the following day. It was a mixed crew. Not a mixed-up crew as some people said. We were officials from the different weekly crews. Those of us who had been around awhile had worked previously with each other. The League office selects the officials that they want to work the play-off games. I had my regular umpire, Joe Connell. All of us were glad to review and discuss rules. It kept us indoors. And warm.

Sunday morning I received my wake-up call. I knew I had a problem. The phone rang and "Good morning. Good morning. Time to get up. It's clear and cold. Twelve below zero and temperature falling fast. Have a good game."

"Have a good game" and "Have a nice day" mean the same. Nothing. At breakfast we discussed the cold weather. None of the officials had gloves or earmuffs. Three of the officials had thermal underwear. We needed more clothes. Fortunately, the owner of a sporting goods store opened his place for us. We bought earmuffs, thermal underwear and thermal socks.

Here's how I walked out onto the field that afternoon to work

the championship game in Green Bay. I had on my usual underwear, two pair of thermal socks besides the football stockings,
thermal underwear—tops and bottoms—turtleneck nylon ski
sweater, plastic Baggies on my feet over my socks to try to keep
my feet warm by keeping the heat in, a large plastic cover that
the cleaners use to return your suits under my football striped
shirt, earmuffs, gloves and my white cap. That white hat was so
people could recognize the good guy on the field.

I still got cold. The extremities—fingertips, toes, nose—just
didn't get warm. Officials go both ways, offensive and defensive,
and never get a substitute. When the game ended, I got the hell
out of there. My left heel became frostbitten and I had a lulu of a
cold for eight days. I wondered what the hell I was doing there. I
felt like Charlie Brown in the comic strip. My biggest worry was
falling down and freezing to death on the ground. I never would
have been able to get up. I know they would have left me there.

Would you believe that the championship game between Green
Bay and Dallas, December 31, 1967, was played without a whistle
being blown all afternoon? Believe it! It was 25 degrees below zero.

I blew my whistle to start the game. It was the last whistle
blown that day. Joe Connell, my umpire, tried to blow his whistle
on the runback of the opening kickoff. All he got was a half soft
tweet-tweet. The wooden balls in our whistles had frozen.

When Connell took the whistle out of his mouth, half of his
lower lip came with it. He wasn't using a nipple on his whistle. All
game long, we yelled, "Stay away," "Keep off him," and "Watch
it." No one knew the difference.

I saw Art Modell, owner of the Cleveland Browns, at the airport after the game. He came up to me and said, "Looked like a
lot of slow whistles today, Norm."

I didn't have the heart to tell him that there were no whistles
that day.

It was hell frozen over. It couldn't have been any colder. The
heated pipes under the turf never did work. They were frozen too.
Everyone was frozen. The players couldn't wait for the game to
end. It was late in the fourth quarter when I spotted the television
relay man wildly waving his hands. He needed a time-out for a
commercial. They were short one. That meant about $150,000

then. It's a lot more now, of course. If they lost that commercial, I might lose my job. Easy come, easy go.

When Green Bay threw an incomplete pass which killed (stopped) the clock, I called a time-out. There were less than four minutes to play. Or freeze. It was so bitter cold. Bob Skoronski, the offensive captain of the Packers, rushed me. "Who the hell called that time out, Norm?"

"I did, Bob. I did, Bob." It was so cold that I said everything twice.

"What the hell for?"

I looked at him and said, "The players' pension fund. The players' pension fund."

"Great call, Norm, great call."

Television was happy. The players' pension fund was happy. I was still freezing and Lombardi was wild. He yelled at me, "Norm, you killed our momentum. You shouldn't have stopped the game. We were on the move. Damn it, damn it. You killed our drive."

Three out of four satisfied people wasn't bad. I figured that's better than one out of two. That's usually the percentage I have when I make a decision. Half for it and half against the call. This time I was three out of four. Television, the players and me against just Lombardi. Just Lombardi?

The finish of the Freeze Bowl game could have been written in Hollywood. Nobody would have believed it could have ended the way it did. Truth is stranger than fiction. At least in this case. There wasn't much time left in the game. About 16 seconds to go. It was third down and only one time left for Green Bay. Bart Starr, the offensive captain for Green Bay, turned to me and said, "Time out, Norm."

I signaled the time-out. That was the Packers' third time-out. That's all any team can get in a half. I had to notify the head coach personally that his team had no more time-outs left. I walked over to Lombardi to give him the word. I looked up at the clock and noticed 16 seconds on the board. I looked at the ball and saw it was resting on Dallas' one-yard line. Perhaps on the two-foot line. Mighty close.

I reached the Packers' bench and saw Lombardi and Starr in deep consultation. They were discussing what to do. I stood by

Lombardi to give him the official word on his team's third time-out. That was it. I overheard a bit of the conversation between Lombardi and Starr. The score at that time was 17–14 in favor of Dallas.

Both men were talking about a field goal. They knew it would tie the score at 17–17. That would force the game into an over-time or sudden death. I just figured I would work the sudden death. I was reviewing my mechanics and procedures in my mind for the sudden-death period. I said to myself, Get the captains of both teams. Toss the coin. Dallas has to call heads or tails as it is the visiting team. They get that option. After the toss, wait three minutes for television and regrouping by both teams. I had it all figured out.

Wrong again. Lombardi turned to me and I said, "Coach, that was your last time-out. No more. Sixteen seconds left to play and it's third down on the two-foot line."

He heard me, and then tuned me out. How that man could concentrate. He turned to Bart Starr and said, "Let's go for it. Try a quarterback sneak."

That's what Starr had suggested. Starr told Lombardi, "You know, we won't have time to get a field goal team in after the play. If we need it."

Lombardi nodded and said, "You won't need it. You are going to score."

Starr ran back to the huddle. Before I signaled the ball ready for play, I went to all of the officials and told them, "Stay alive. Be awake. Keep on your toes. No more time-outs for Green Bay. Side men watch that damn goal line. If it's in, signal touchdown right away. Don't guess. Give it a good look. We're going to earn our pay on this one play. Heads up."

I ran back to my position. I thought to myself, How in hell do I always wind up in this kind of a situation? What a bitch. Here it comes down to one play. And I'm going to be smack in the middle of it. If Starr doesn't get the touchdown, no Dallas player will get off him. If I stop the clock after the play to haul the Dallas play-ers off him, it just might be enough time for Green Bay to get its field goal team lined up for a field goal. If I don't kill the clock to pull the Dallas players off Starr, he never will get up in time to possibly get in another play. What a helluva spot for me.

Starr went over Jerry Kramer's guard position. Kramer drove
Jethro Pugh, the Dallas defensive tackle, back a wee bit. Just
enough to give Starr room to fall over the goal line. I didn't have
to do anything. Just signal the touchdown. And listen to the fans
screaming. There is absolutely no truth to the rumor that I pushed
Bart Starr over the goal line. No way. Not even to get out of a
ticklish situation.

It was the year after the Freeze Bowl. I was back in Green Bay
working a ball game. Henry Jordan, the fine defensive tackle of
the Packers, told me what had happened to Coach Vince Lombardi after the Freeze Bowl game had ended. I can well understand what he meant, for I had thought I was a frozen block of ice
for a week after the game.

Coach Lombardi had stayed around Lambeau Field in Green
Bay long after that game had ended. The fans all had left. Lom-
bardi listened a long time to everyone tell him how great he was.
He started to believe it. His wife, Marie, had gone home earlier as
she was so cold. Lombardi didn't get home until after midnight.
His wife had already gone to bed.

Vince Lombardi was still cold. He went to bed and one of his
cold feet touched his wife's foot. She shot up in bed and said, "My
God, your foot is cold."

Coach Lombardi was still thinking of all the wonderful things
he had heard, answered, "You may call me Vince."

Let me tell you what happened to me once. Weather has never
really been a problem for me. I mean flying in and out the League
cities. Just once. That was in Pittsburgh.

I was weathered-in in Pittsburgh the tail end of a season a few
years back. I called my wife. "Charlotte, my plane is grounded.
Don't bother trying to meet my flight. I'll call you tomorrow
morning when I get back to Los Angeles. Okay?"

After dinner at the hotel in Pittsburgh, I decided to fly out if I
could. I could. I flew into Kansas City, waited a few hours, and
then flew back to Los Angeles. I arrived there around two o'clock
in the morning. I caught a cab home, as I wouldn't ask my wife to
pick me up at that hour. She wouldn't anyway.

I undressed in another room and went to bed. My wife was
lying on the right side of the bed, and I got into bed from the left

side. As she was lying on her right side, my foot accidentally touched her foot.

Without turning around she asked, "Is that you, Norm?"

Who the hell did she think it was? I've never been weathered in since.

My wife has always taken me over to the airport and picked me up when I returned from a ball game. It beats the hassle of parking and fighting the traffic. It's a lot more convenient, especially as we live near the airport. Early in my refereeing career I flew home from Washington, D.C. Few passengers were on that flight, so the stewardesses had lots of time for the few passengers.

After I had picked up my luggage and was putting it into our car, three of the stewardesses walked past us. They happily yelled, "Hi, Norm. See you next week."

I nodded and said, "Sure thing. See you Pam, Susan, Sharon. Nice to fly with you."

On the drive home from the airport my wife glanced over. "Who were those three young girls? You certainly knew them. And you knew all their names too."

"No problem learning their names. You see, when you enter the plane, right on the wall inside, there is a list of the names of the captain of the plane and the stewardesses. That's how I know their names."

My wife drove on for a second, then, "What's the captain's name?"

To get back to Vince Lombardi, the big thing with him was integrity, honesty, hard work and preparation. That's what made a winner.

We were in Green Bay one Thanksgiving Day. Minnesota was there with me. It was nationally televised, and you may remember the play. Fran Tarkenton was scrambling all over the field before he threw the ball. I had a swing man filling in for my regular umpire that day. A swing man is an extra official the League had at that time who replaced a different man each week. This week was my turn to have him. I walked over to him and said, "Dick, watch for ineligible men downfield. Tarkenton is taking a helluva long time to get rid of the ball. One of the linemen might be moving downfield a bit. Keep your eyes on those offensive interior linemen." It is illegal for linemen to go downfield before the ball is thrown on a forward pass play. They sneak down occasionally, especially if the quarterback scrambles.

Dick nodded and I started the next play. Tarkenton took the snap, fell back to throw and couldn't spot an eligible receiver. He scrambled all over the backfield. Finally, he threw the ball.

I looked downfield. Sure enough, the umpire's flag was on the ground. Dick had spotted an ineligible man downfield. Dick ran up to me and said, "I got a lineman downfield. Number Seventy-seven." He pointed to the tackle, #77. Dick was so proud. Real pleased with himself.

I turned to see #77, the tackle. It was a tackle, but it was a defensive tackle. He could go wherever he damn pleased. I said, "Number Seventy-seven is a defensive man. He's not an ineligible man. Pick up your flag. No foul."

He did pick it up. Quickly too. Not quick enough. Coach Lombardi was shouting. I went over to him and he said, "I saw the flag. It's a foul. If there is a flag down, there is a foul. We want the penalty that was called on Number Seventy-seven."

"Coach, it was a mistake. He had the wrong team."

Lombardi looked at me as if I were out of my mind. He nodded and walked away. He gave me a shot and when it didn't work, he forgot it. There's the difference between a winner and a loser. The losers never stop arguing, never forget, and always think you "jobbed" them. They didn't come any finer or better than Vince Lombardi.

Lombardi's last year as a coach was with the Washington Redskins. They were in Baltimore playing the Colts. I was refereeing the game. Lombardi might have been pulling my leg, but he sure sounded like he meant it. Washington had kicked off to start the game, and the kickoff went over the end line for an automatic touchback. I put the ball on the 20-yard line and signaled a first down and 10 yards to go.

On the first play the Colts ran the ball out to the 25-yard line stripe. That was a gain of five yards. On the next play the Redskins were off side. That meant another five yards against Lombardi's team. I picked up the ball, measured off the five yards to the 30-yard line, put the ball down and signaled first down. No problem.

It wasn't that easy. Coach Lombardi was waving his hands and yelling for my attention. He got it. I walked over to him. "What do you want, Coach?"

"I want a measurement. It may not be a first down," he shouted.

"Not a first down? Coach, the ball is right on the thirty-yard stripe. We started from the twenty-yard line, and that is ten yards back. That's a first down. What do you want with a measurement?"

He stared at me, the way Lombardi always did. It was a stare. "We're entitled to a measurement if we ask for it. I'm asking. The stripes and lines may be marked wrong. Maybe not five yards apart. It may be marked wrong. Maybe not five yards apart. It may be short."

I saw then that it wasn't going to be my day. "Well, Coach, if it's wrong for the Colts, it's going to be the same for you. It's a first down today. No measurement."

Maybe Lombardi was remembering a game I worked in Chicago. It was a hard-fought game between the Packers and the Bears. They always are. The game was a close one. The score was tied and the Bears had the ball, first down around their 49-yard line. The Packers were off side and it was called. I picked up the ball, made a mental note that the ball had been on the 49-yard line and then ran to the new spot. I crossed the midfield stripe and placed the ball down. I gave the ready-to-play signal, and moved back to my referee's position.

As Billy Wade was barking signals, the game announcer said, "First down and three yards to go."

First down and three yards to go. I had walked off seven yards instead of five yards. Instead of placing the ball on the yard stripe before the 45-yard line marker, I placed it past the 45-yard line. The ball was resting on the 44-yard line rather than the 46-yard line.

I tried to stop the play but the center snapped the ball before I could blow my whistle. Wade threw a completed pass for 20 yards. Good thing it was a pass. If the Bears had run the ball and made three yards, I would have had a problem. A tough one. Would it have been a first down or would I have done something else? I'm glad that I didn't have that decision to make.

On the way off the field, Coach Lombardi told me, "You owe

me two yards. Save it for me. I'll need it sometime when we're close to the goal line."

He never bitched about it during the game. Or after the game. He had me cold, but Lombardi was a real pro.

Lombardi's teams seldom fouled. He saw to it. I don't mean by intimidating the officials. He got after his players. He'd let them know when they fouled, and how much it hurt the team. That's why if you check the penalty statistics of the Green Bay Packers during his regime, you will find that his team fouled very seldom and was usually the least penalized team in the League.

I remember watching a Packers practice one year at their training camp. I had gone there to give them a rules talk before the season started. Bart Starr, one of the game's most publicized quarterbacks and a deserving one, was working the team in a drill. They were timing the offensive team to see if it would get the ball off in allowed 30 seconds. On one play it took 32 seconds to take the snap from the center, Jim Ringo. Lombardi stopped play immediately and told Starr, "Cut the time down. The delay penalty might cost us a game during the season. Get that play off before thirty seconds."

Bart Starr nodded. No big scene, no fuss, no histrionics. Just solid coaching. I'll bet if you check, Starr was seldom, if ever, called for a 30-second delay. What a difference from the coaches whose teams "never foul." The officials always screw them. At least that's what they say.

When I give a rules talk, I review the new rules, go over the old rules, and discuss what the officials look for in the way of fouls. That's followed by a question-answer period. Some teams do a great job with the rules talks. Other teams go through the motions. I notice that the ones that do not listen too carefully usually are the teams that foul the most. At least that's what the penalty statistics show at the end of every year.

Green Bay trains at St. Norbert College, a small Catholic college in DePere, Wisconsin, just outside of Green Bay. It has very nice facilities. Lombardi ran a hard-nosed camp. All work, no nonsense, and tough conditioning. His teams were always ready and in shape. I spoke to the team at one o'clock one afternoon. Right after lunch, and after they had had a blistering morning workout.

They were still on the two-a-day routine. Bart Starr, Paul Hornung, Jim Taylor, Willie Davis, Gerry Kramer and all the others listened. Carefully too. When Vince Lombardi listened, everybody listened.

As I was talking, I noticed a rookie in the second row fighting hard to keep his eyes open. He couldn't do it. His head was flopping over every second or so. The rookie was tired, nervous, frightened and eager to make the team. Also sleepy. Coach Lombardi spotted the rookie dozing off. That's the same as robbing a bank. At least to the coach. Lombardi pointed his finger at him and said, "Norm, ask him a question."

I pretended not to hear Coach Lombardi. I just raised my voice, hoping the rookie would hear it and snap awake. A rules talk is not the most stimulating or interesting thing in the world. Even when I give it. Or especially when I give it. Not when you are tired and worried about a job. Such as making the Packers.

Lombardi almost stood up in his seat. "Norm, ask him a question."

No way. I wasn't trying to make the team. I wasn't going to ask him a question. He wouldn't hear me. Lombardi asked me one more time to ask that question. Much louder. That startled the rookie. I never asked the question. The rookie never had to answer the question. He was gone the next day.

Vince Lombardi was not inclined to pick on rookies. He was the same with everyone. I remember a game Green Bay had with Dallas in the Cotton Bowl one Thanksgiving Day. The Packers were ahead and were trying to run out the clock. Dallas had used up their allotted three time-outs that half. It was just a question of letting the clock run out. For some unknown reason, Green Bay's defensive captain, who was a cornerback, yelled to me, "Hey, Ref. Time out."

I looked around. I thought Dallas was trying to run one by getting me to stop the clock. No way could I do that. Unless I blew it. And I have done that too. As I turned, the defensive captain yelled again, "Ref, time out. I want it."

I signaled the time-out. It stopped the clock. That's what Dallas wanted. Not Lombardi. He stormed the sideline, gesturing to me. I saw his mouth open, his eyes alive, so I walked over to him. He screamed at me, "What the hell are you calling time out for? You can't give Dallas an extra time-out. What's the matter with you?"

Coach, I didn't give Dallas a time-out. Your defensive captain did. He called time out."

"What" he shouted. With that he left me and yelled to his defensive captain, "Did you call time out?"

"I sure did," came back the reply.

At least I was off the hook. Lombardi almost came out on the field after his captain. "What for? I didn't want a time-out."

The player looked at Lombardi. "I was tired. It's hot. I'm playing and you're not."

Oh-oh. Lombardi looked, turned and didn't say a word. The player, a good one, was gone within a week. Probably within 48 hours. What I am saying is that there was only one head man when Lombardi was coaching. That was Lombardi. Whether it was a rookie or a veteran star, he was the boss. A real boss. A pro all the way. Yes, I liked Vince Lombardi. He was fair, he was honest, he was consistent and he was damn good. That's a hard combination to beat.

Did you ever wonder why the goalposts are now 30 feet above the crossbar? Rather than the 10 feet they had been for over 40 years? It all resulted from a controversial call in the championship game between the Green Bay Packers and the Baltimore Colts. Lombardi was coach of the Packers, Shula coach of the Colts, and I was the referee in the middle of the whole damn affair. This is one time that I can honestly say that I was wrongly badgered. I had nothing to do with it, but there I was. Right in the middle.

It happened in the fourth quarter after I had given both coaches the two-minute warning before the end of the game. It was fourth down and the ball was resting on the Colts' 22-yard line with the Colts leading by a score of 10–7. Don Chandler trotted out onto the field and took his spot behind the place-kick holder, Bart Starr. Starr was kneeling on the 29-yard line so it was well within Chandler's kicking range. The goalposts then were located on the goal line, not on the end line as they are today. The ball was snapped to Starr, who placed it on the ground, and Chandler came across with his right leg and the ball was up. The ball sailed toward the goalposts and went about 20 or more feet above the right post (upright), which was only 10 feet above the crossbar. Green Bay knew it was good. Baltimore knew it was no good. The ball couldn't have been in or out by more than an inch or two. Jim Tunney, the field judge then, knew it was good. There was no question in his mind. And he was the only one who counted. It was his call and he was in the best spot in the stadium to see it and to call it. He stood a bit back of the goalposts so he had a great look at it. A real tough call. Very close. But not a doubt in Tunney's mind. He raised his hands. Successful kick. That tied the score at 10–10. That sent the game into overtime. And Chandler kicked the winning score after 13 minutes and 33 seconds had gone by in the fifth quarter. That was the longest overtime in the NFL since the 1958 game when Baltimore beat the New York Giants.

Chuck Thompson, the Colts' fine announcer, wasn't too happy about the call. He thought that I had made it, for I gave the signal that it was good. He didn't realize all I did was pick up the field judge's signal from under the goalposts. And he had signaled good. They tell me that for three months after the game Thompson ended his nightly sports show with "And good night, Norm Schachter, wherever you are."

The next year the Rules Committee passed a resolution. It stated that all goalpost uprights would extend 30 feet above the crossbar and would be no less than 3 inches and no more than 4 inches in diameter. A ribbon 4 inches by 42 inches was to be attached to the top of each post. Since then I have had quite a number of balls on field goal attempts hit the upright high on the extended post and fall back onto the field. That made it easy to call it no good. I hate to think of having to make that call now without those extensions. Those extensions just might have changed some League winners, I'm sure. We now also have two men under the goalposts to get a better look. When you go to a game now and look at a field goal attempt, just remember that the entire ball has to be inside the vertical line indicated by the outer edge of the goalpost while the ball is passing over the top of the goalpost. Not too easy to call a tight one, is it?

What really had created all the heated discussion on Chandler's controversial call was Chandler himself. His reaction after he had kicked the ball stirred up the bitterness. Chandler had looked downfield just after he had kicked the ball. He saw the ball go over the goalpost. He shook his head as if he had missed the kick. TV picked up that movement of his head. Why he did that, I will never understand.

The next year Don Chandler told me, "Coach Lombardi really told me. He said that I wasn't the official downfield. I didn't have to make the call. That's why they pay the field judge. If I was going to show any emotion, jump around as if it was good. Signal good. All the time. Never no good when I kick it. Give the officials help, but only helping us."

There's that fair advantage Vince Lombardi always wanted.

Green Bay was a nice place to work. But it was tough to get out of there. The last plane for Chicago left Green Bay at 4:25 P.M. The game started at 1:00 P.M., so that meant a very tight connection. If we missed that plane, it was all night in Green Bay. That's not bad, except I worked in Los Angeles Monday morning.

We officials had a good thing going for us. Coach Lombardi had arranged it. After we had dressed following the game, a police car hustled us to the airport. Without such help, we didn't have a chance to make the flight.

After a tough loss for Green Bay one Sunday afternoon, the fans were excited. Excited means that they were mad as hell at us. When we had showered, dressed and jumped into the police car, the police put on the sirens and red lights as they drove away from the stadium toward the airport. I can still hear the shouts that Sunday afternoon. When we started to leave the stadium in the police car, the fans screamed and yelled, "That's right, officers. We saw the game. They're robbers. They stole the game. Lock them up. Take them away."

We missed the flight. Maybe the fans were right for a change. It was the only time that I can ever remember missing the 4:25 P.M. flight.

Sure, Lombardi chewed me out. I wasn't any different. He also told me, "You worked a good game, Norm." Said that even when he lost the game. I never heard a foul word come out of Vince Lombardi's mouth.

John Madden

John Madden, the former Oakland Raiders coach, was unbelievable. You had to see him and work with him to believe him.
He looked wild on the sidelines. Not wild like a bear, more like a
walrus. He was bigger than most players and he was on center
stage all the time. He thought the referee and the other officials
were part of his team. He yelled instructions to us like he did to
his players, he chewed us out like he did his players, and sometimes he praised us like he did his players. But never on a call
against his team. I think he was one helluva coach. His win record
bears that out. He seemed to have a closer relationship with his
players than most of the other coaches. Al Davis, the managing
general partner of Oakland, picked up players who had been
dropped from other clubs. These players, who couldn't get along
and were hell raisers and indifferent to discipline, all seemed to
find a home with Madden in Oakland. Somehow Coach Madden
got them to shape up. He never had a problem with them. He
must have been doing something right.

Madden reminded me of Puck, Shakespeare's character in *A
Midsummer Night's Dream*. Puck was a mischievous fellow who
was a shrewd sprite of a big elf. Madden was always putting on
the referee. He was angry one minute, smiling one minute, upset
another minute and vocal the other 57 minutes of a ball game. He
may have had the best sense of humor of any winning coach in
the National Football League. Or any league. He kept a referee

on his toes. He had that needle out all the time. About a foot long. And he was always looking for that fair advantage. Oh, boy, did he look for that fair advantage. I got more than my share of laughs from John Madden. His sense of humor kept a referee loose enough when he was working an Oakland Raiders game. Their games were always tough, never routine. I liked Madden. Even when he lambasted me on the field. They don't come much better than John Madden. Or funnier. Madden is still a very funny man. Vocal too. Catch his act the next time you watch his calm-excited routine in his beer commercial. Who's excited!

It was a hot afternoon in Oakland. Madden was all over the sideline, gesticulating on every play, and screaming at Jack Fette, our line judge. Fette was not one to scream at. He screamed back. I was glad when the game ended. About 15 minutes after the game had ended, Madden knocked on our dressing room door. He asked if he could talk to me. I told him he could if he didn't come any farther than the doorway. It didn't matter for he talked loud.

The officials were all undressed and waiting their turn to shower. Fette had just finished his shower. He had a large towel around his waist as he walked back to his dressing cubicle.

When the door opened, Madden peeked in. He stayed in the doorway. He spotted Fette and started on him. Madden got it off his chest. Fette stared at him, turned his back to Madden and dropped his towel, which was around his waist. There was Fette, stark naked, bending over at the waist with his ass facing Madden.

Madden didn't even break stride. He stared at Fette's rear end and said, "And that goes for you too, Schachter."

People still ask me about a Denver-Oakland game a few years ago. It always comes up when I speak to any group. It was in Denver, and it was a typical Denver-Oakland game. Hard and tough. Especially to work. It was a nationally televised game, so it got tremendous coverage.

It was a tight ball game. Madden was all over the sidelines, trying for his fair advantage. He's a combination of Halas and Lombardi: Halas' expressions, language and actions along with Lombardi's determination, desire to win, hard-nosed attitude and inner toughness. On this particular play a Broncos runner, Floyd

Little, ran 10 or 15 yards and then ran out of bounds just before he was tackled. One of Oakland's corner linebackers came up and flipped Little on his ass after he was out of bounds. That's a no-no. That's a foul. When a runner crosses the sideline, no one is supposed to tackle him for he is out of bounds and the play is already over. He can't go anywhere.

Fette, the line judge, was right on the play. He always is. He's an excellent official. His flag hit the ground before Floyd Little did. That meant another 15 yards tacked onto the end of the run. It was an unnecessary-roughness foul. I stepped out in the open, flipped on my microphone and announced to the country, "Unnecessary roughness on the defense. Fifteen yards and a first down for Denver."

I looked over to the sidelines and Coach Madden was having a few words with Fette. I hated to see it. Fette is not the man to blast. Before long, I saw Fette throw his flag again. This time real high. I didn't even go over to Fette to ask what the flag was for. I knew. I just put on my microphone again and said, "Unsportsmanlike conduct on the defense. Fifteen yards."

I stepped off the total 30 yards, 15 for unnecessary roughness on Little and 15 yards for unsportsmanlike conduct on Madden. Do you realize how much 30 yards are in a tough ball game? Madden was beside himself. Screaming, yelling and wild. He wanted me to come over to see him. As time was out, I walked over toward his bench. I walked by Jack Fette. As I neared Fette, I said, "Jack, what did he call you? I know he must have called you something bad."

Fette was standing on the inbounds hash mark with his hands folded and staring across the field. He didn't even turn his head but said, "He called me a blind bastard. Twice."

I kept walking toward Madden and finally reached him. I never run over to a coach when he wants me. It will wait until I get there. It did. Madden greeted me with "Shit, Norm, what the hell was the last foul for?"

Picture this scene: Madden and me. On national television. Fortunately, I checked to make certain that my microphone was off. "Coach, the fifteen-yard penalty for unsportsmanlike conduct was on you."

"On me? What the hell for? I didn't say anything."

"Yes, you did. Coach. You called Fette a blind bastard. He resents that. That's fifteen yards."

"I didn't call him a blind bastard. I called him a no-good bastard."

"Oh, no, Coach. You called him a blind bastard. Not once, but twice. That's what Fette says. He never lies to me."

"Hell. He asked me what I had said. I repeated it. What the hell did he ask me to repeat it for, if he didn't want me to say it? Shit, that word I called him is the same as darn and gosh now, isn't it?"

"Coach, Fette was giving you a chance to back off when he asked you if you were speaking to him. You didn't want to. That cost fifteen yards. He hoped you would say you weren't talking to him, but to one of your players. You didn't want to back off, so it's fifteen."

I turned away and ran back to my position on the field. On my way back I passed Fette, who was still standing in the same spot, with his hands folded across his chest. As I passed him, I said, "Fette, you're a no-good blind bastard." He smiled. This time he kept his flag in his pocket.

Funny how similar situations tend to repeat themselves. When I was still working high school games years ago, many years ago, I was assigned to referee a strange combination of teams. It was a game between Black-Fox Military Academy, a got-rocks school, and the Whittier School for Boys, a school for delinquent young boys. Two different groups of boys. In speech, mannerisms, attitude and viewpoints.

During the first quarter, a lineman for the Whittier School for Boys, a tackle with #72 on his shirt, kept trying to scare the nice young man from Black-Fox who was playing opposite him. He kept saying, "I'm going to kick the shit out of this rich bastard."

I heard it a second time and stepped right in and looked at #72. "Listen, Number Seventy-two, watch your language. Clean up your act. Knock off the dirty talk. Play ball and keep your talk clean, as well as your hands."

Number Seventy-two walked up to me, looked up and asked, "Dirty talk? What dirty talk? I didn't say anything dirty."

"You said 'shit' and 'bastard.' Knock it off."

"Shit and bastard? Are those dirty words?"

I looked at him, realized they weren't to him, and yelled, "Let's play ball."

Coach Madden and I were talking before the game one Sunday afternoon. That was the best time to talk to Madden. Before the game he was calm, agreeable and pleasant. During the game he played a different role as the score changed and penalties were called.

For some reason George Blanda was not having another of his miraculous games. The season before, he took Oakland to victory five weeks in a row in a string of the greatest one-man performances imaginable. He drove Oakland to victories over Cleveland and Denver in the final minutes of the games. In the last seconds of the game against Kansas City he had kicked a 48-yard field goal for the winning score.

Madden and I watched Blanda doing his pre-game warm-ups. I turned to Madden. "That guy keeps rolling along. I remember him with the Chicago Bears in the fifties. He sure has made a great coach out of you."

Madden grinned as I walked away.

George Blanda had a fabulous career. He deserved everything nice that happened to him. He never was a problem and he kept his feet solidly on the ground. Even that day in Oakland when Blanda wasn't having one of his super days. Either the blocking assignments on pass protection for him were breaking down or he was taking too long to throw the ball. Blanda was being sacked too often. He was having a difficult time trying to stay on his feet. The pass rush was brutal.

Prior to the game I had talked with Blanda. His biography had just come out to capitalize on his popularity, which was at an all-time high. We had discussed writing and stories. But now it was different. The game was on. After a particular hard sack, Blanda looked over at me. Before he could say anything, I asked him, "George, don't forget I want you to autograph that book of yours."

If I remember correctly, he told me what to do with the book.

Coach Madden's assistant coaches were all out of the same mold. His. Ollie Spencer, a fine offensive coach for the Raiders, got excited once in a while. Once in a while was 59 minutes out of 60. But he was sharp. Funny too.

We were working in Oakland one Sunday. Not a bad ball game. I only heard Ollie Spencer yell five times that day. All on plays that happened in front of me. Stuff like intentional grounding of the ball, roughing the passer, running into the kicker—stuff like that. All my calls. I had five that day. There was also an offensive holding against one of Oakland's offensive tackles. All against Oakland. Oakland won anyway.

After the game there was a knock on our dressing room door. I opened the door and there was Ollie Spencer, with a football in his hand. He looked over at me and said, "Here's the game ball, Norm. Our team and Coach Madden voted to give you the game ball. You gained more yardage than all our runners combined. You were the most consistent one out on the field today. You were one hundred percent. You missed every call you made. You were perfect. No one on our team was close to that. Here's the ball."

You would have had to see it to believe it. I was there, saw it and still have trouble believing it ever happened. It certainly was a first. At least to our crew.

The crew was in Oakland. Gerry Hart, the umpire, had a couple of holding calls against the Raiders. Ollie Spencer and Hart had played ball together in Detroit years ago. They were friends, but not that day. In fact, there is no room for friendship when you're officiating a football game. Spencer got after Hart. It was vicious, but Gerry couldn't hear too much of what was said. Finally, after a touchdown Hart went to his position on the kicking team's 45-yard line. It was on Oakland's side. And Spencer really went after Hart. He let him have it verbally. I heard it down under the goalposts where I was standing.

Hart heard enough. He turned to Spencer and barked at him, "Ollie, that's all. You've had your say. Now knock it off. Any more out of you and it will cost you fifteen yards. Quiet down and get off my back."

I was just about to blow my whistle for the kickoff. Before I could, Spencer walked onto the field about five yards and was in front of Hart and the Oakland players on the sideline. He raised his hands high above his shoulders. I held my whistle, for if I had blown it, Spencer would have been rushed out by the rush of players moving over him. I listened to what Ollie had to say from his spot out on the field.

"Listen, all of you. I want to tell you something. If any of you, any of you, ever have a friend who becomes a football official, drop him. He is no damn fuckin' good. He's a sonavabitch. Drop him."

I looked at Hart. He didn't throw his flag. He was laughing too hard. So was I. So were the Oakland players. Not Spencer though, he meant it.

One year I went up to Santa Rosa to give Oakland a rules talk during pre-season training. That's one rules talk I always enjoy. It was a grab-ass affair. I usually speak and answer questions for about an hour. Sometimes less, sometimes more. Many veteran players feel as if they can do without my rules talk. This particular time it was held on a Saturday night. The team was still on a two-a-day workout practice routine. Santa Rosa is a warm city, so the fellows had had a tough day. It was one of the few Saturday nights they would be free, except for my rules talk. The club had a movie lined up for them. When I walked into the room, there was the usual blackboard in the front. I used it occasionally to illustrate a rule. On the blackboard was this note:

Dear Norm:

We are going to a movie at 6:30 P.M. That's 30 minutes from now.

The Team

I looked at the note. I was to start at six and go for an hour. Supposedly. Madden was sitting there. I picked up the chalk, drew a line under the team's signature and wrote:

Dear Team:

So am I.
Norm

The rules talk took an hour anyway. The questions by the players and coaches are always stimulating in Oakland's camp. Before I started my talk, one of the coaches told me that they had been reviewing films earlier in the day. They were confused about a ruling on a backward pass play that had occurred. They wanted me to go over the backward pass. No problem.

"Fellows," I began, "I want to go over the backward pass and everything that can happen on that pass. First, let me tell you what a backward pass is. A backward pass is any pass that is not forward."

Gene Upshaw, who comes in at 6 feet 5 inches and 265 pounds and who is the offensive captain of the Raiders, raised his hand and said, "Norm, do you want to go over that again?"

That needle was always prodding.

Miami had a winning streak on the line when they came into Oakland one Sunday afternoon for a game with the Raiders. It was on national television. I had to stop the game for three long minutes when a vicious-looking police dog ran onto the field. It was the first time that afternoon that Madden and Shula had nothing to say. It was that big of a police dog. Biggest one I had ever seen. On the loose.

There are two things a referee learns early in his career. One is never to take a ball away from a kid who runs onto the field and grabs the football. I once did. My ears are still ringing. The fans really let me have it. The other no-no is never to chase a dog that wanders onto the field. Especially a large police dog. They have a man assigned to that job.

The large police dog took over the game. He ran all over the place. Three security men were right on his tail, but he was a great open-field runner. Finally, the dog had had enough. He stopped right on the 50-yard line in the middle of the field and showed everybody in the country what he thought of my refereeing. Security collared him there.

I got a letter the following Tuesday. Here it is.

FEDERAL MEDIATION AND CONCILIATION BOARD
UNITED STATES GOVERNMENT
450 Golden Gate Avenue, Box 37667
San Francisco, California 94102

Dear #56:

I thought you did your usual game, both teams were mad at you. It looks as if you are slowing down a bit from the last game I watched you work. At least it appears that way from my living room. I don't see how that is possible.

Cordially yours,
Lowell McGinnis
Regional Director

P.S. By the way, which one of the officials let their seeing-eye dog on the field?

Coach Madden was one of the brightest in professional football. Yesterday. And also today. He had a great organization. He knew how to get the most out of his players, how and where to use them, and had an excellent rapport with his entire squad and fellow coaches. He was extremely dedicated, especially to winning and getting his fair advantage. He was overenthusiastic and was a cheerleader. Sometimes his enthusiasm got him involved with the game officials. Madden didn't carry grudges. It started all over again every Sunday during the season. That's the way it should be. He had and still has that great sense of humor. I like that.

Tom Landry

Tom Landry is one of a kind. Never changes expression, standing there on the sideline, wearing his nice hat, sports jacket, often looking at a program he holds in his left hand. He never seems to say a word. Never yells at an official and I never heard him swear. Not even hell or damn, not to anyone on the field. He doesn't have to. He's the only coach I've known who doesn't needle. Maybe Mike Ditka or Ernie Stautner, two of his assistant coaches, do it for him. His team does it for him out on the field. Gil Brandt, the great talent scout of the Cowboys, occasionally growls at a referee.

I've seen Landry get some of the toughest breaks in football. I have refereed games where nothing went right for him or his team. Green Bay barely beat them several times for championships. Those games could have gone either way. The breaks just didn't go Coach Landry's way. Like the championship game where Dallas scored the winning touchdown and the tackle was off side a wee bit. Brought the ball back with a five-yard penalty. Dallas never did score. Then there was the Freeze Bowl game. They almost had that one too. And Super Bowl V and Super Bowl X, both of which I refereed, could have gone their way with a few breaks. But they didn't get them. Still, there was never a complaint about the officiating.

What I am saying is that Tom Landry acts the same to the referee win or lose. It may eat his insides out, but he doesn't put the monkey on the referee's back. He became head coach of the Cowboys in 1960, and he's still there. Tex Schramm, president and general manager, and Clint Murchison, chairman of the board and owner of the team, must know how good Landry is. There's never any talk of firing him. There shouldn't be. I think he's great. Both as a coach and a person. He's a helluva coach. His record shows that. He's a helluva person. His actions show that.

I remember when Dallas came into the National Football League. They weren't too strong. Thin in many positions. Didn't have the top-quality players they have today. Not enough of them anyway. When Dallas entered the NFL in 1960, they had a scheduled pre-season game with the Los Angeles Rams in Pendleton, Oregon, at the famous Roundup fairgrounds. When we officials arrived at the rodeo fairgrounds, we couldn't find a place to suit up for the game. Apparently, a football officials' dressing room was the one thing that they didn't need or have. I asked Coach Landry if he knew where we officials dressed. He shook his head. I asked Bob Waterfield, the Rams' coach, where we dressed. He also shook his head. They had their own problems. As the hour of the game kept getting closer and closer, I became a bit nervous when I couldn't find a place to undress and put on my striped shirt and short pants. I finally corraled (that's the right word, believe me) one of the policemen working at the field.

"Say, Officer, I need a little help. I'm the referee and I don't know where we're supposed to dress for the game. Do you know where the officials' dressing room would be?"

The officer scratched his chin for a few seconds. "You know, this is a rodeo field. I don't know if there is a dressing room for football officials."

I was really nervous then. "I know that it's a rodeo field. But could you check it out for me? They must have made some arrangements."

He took off. He was gone for almost five terrible minutes. Finally, he came back and told me, "I don't know where you dress. But you come out of chute number three."

Once, just once, did I see Coach Tom Landry show emotion. Openly, that is. Out on the field. It was at another one of those "on the edge of your seats" games. The New York Giants were in great position. They were behind Dallas by two points, but they were on Dallas' five-yard line, fourth down with 20 seconds to play. Pete Gogolak would come in, kick the field goal, and the Giants would win by one point. A piece of cake.

Gogolak did come in. He kicked the ball from the Dallas 12-yard line. Bob Lilly, the huge tackle from Dallas, came in and jumped up into the path of the kicked ball. Then I saw the greatest reaction by a player that I have ever seen. Gogolak turned sideways and kicked the ball again with his other foot, the left one, as the ball came toward him on a bounce after it had hit Lilly's chest. It was a bang-bang play. The ball went over the crossbar. I looked around, saw the Giant players jumping up and down and heard the roar of the crowd. 62,892 excited fans were on their feet, waving their hands and signaling "We're number one." That's when I threw my flag. The Giants rushed me. All of them. It looked like a hundred, but I know it couldn't be more than eleven of them.

"What's the flag for, Norm? What's the penalty flag for?"

I told them, "I don't know, but I know it's wrong."

It was a gut reaction. Instinctive, maybe. Maybe it was the experience of over 400 professional football games.

When I spoke to the two captains, I had it all figured out. You can't kick a loose ball. And that's what the blocked kick was. It was a loose ball. Not only that, but I gave the ball to Dallas on their 20-yard line. The ball had gone over the end line for a touchback and I automatically gave Dallas the ball rather than the choice of the penalty.

I can still hear and see Don Meredith, the quarterback for Dallas, come running out and with his Texan drawl say, "Great call, great call. What was it?"

"Touchback, Don. Don't talk anymore. Get a play in and get the game over. And let's get the hell out of here. Alive."

Every time I see Meredith now he tells me what a great call that was. To this day, he has no idea what I had called. Or cares.

But it did bring a full smile to Tom Landry's face as he ran off the field.

As stoical as Tom Landry seems out on the field, I do remember another half-smile incident. And I was the butt of the situation, literally and figuratively. Remember how cold I told you the weather was that day in Green Bay for the Freeze Bowl? Well, it was just the opposite one night in Dallas at the Cotton Bowl. Dallas was playing Minnesota a pre-season game. The temperature was 100 degrees straight up when I blew my whistle to start the football game. The humidity was just as bad. It was sweltering that night and nothing seemed to be going right for Dallas. Or for the officials. Blocks were missed, balls were fumbled, passes were dropped and I'm sure the Cowboys thought the referee's calls were not too good. Maybe they were right. But Coach Landry never said a word. At least not to me.

He might have said something to Ernie Stautner, his defensive coordinator. You have to know Stautner. He was a great, great defensive tackle for the Pittsburgh Steelers for 14 years. And I mean great. I liked him when he was playing. I still do, for he always helps me. He tried then and he tries now. Always has something to say. I remember talking to him early that hot night when an incident came up near the Dallas bench. Ernie let out a growl. I turned to him and said, "Is that you, Stautner? Yes, it is. Damn it. I didn't recognize you without that arm cast on."

Stautner had played 14 years in Pittsburgh with an arm cast on his left arm. At least it seemed that way to the officials. They joked how he took it off on Monday and put it back on again on Sunday morning for the game. He never misused the cast though, I mean as a club in fending off those offensive tackles. If he had, the officials would have run his ass off the field.

It was a first down measurement right by the Dallas Cowboys' bench near the sideline. It was close, very close. I bent over to give it a good look, straddled my legs far apart so I could bend over easier, and wham—my pants ripped down the seam in the rear. It was a good wide rip. And I wasn't wearing anything under my football pants as it was so damn unbearably hot and humid.

Before I could straighten up, Ernie Stautner, who was standing behind me, watching me bend over to measure for a possible first down, saw the rip. The first thing I heard was Stautner saying, "Norm, that's the most you've shown me all day."

Landry gave me a half-smile.

I remember Super Bowl V, which I refereed. Coach Tom Landry showed me what the word professional means. Super Bowl games have lots of pressures. Fortunately, game pressures never got to me. The only time I ever worried was when quarterbacks would run the clock down in the last 20 seconds before they would call a time-out. They wanted only enough time to kick the field goal and have the clock run out. This would prevent the other team from getting the ball back that half. It was nervous time for me.

Super Bowl V had one of those clock-running-down situations. Baltimore had the ball on the Dallas 25-yard line with less than 30 seconds left in the ball game. With the score tied 13–13, Earl Morrall, quarterback and the offensive captain of the Colts, came over to stand with me. He was going to let the clock run down to a couple of seconds and then call a time-out. No way did he want Dallas to get the ball again.

However, it became nervous time. The Colt players were afraid that time would run out before Morrall could call the time-out. They kept telling him, "Call time out, call time out." I could only take the time-out request from the designated captain. Morrall didn't wait as long as he should have, and at nine seconds remaining he called time out.

After the time-out was called and taken, Jim O'Brien came in to kick the field goal. Dallas then asked for a time-out. I didn't allow it. You can't have two consecutive time-outs. The Cowboys wanted O'Brien to have some extra time to think. Perhaps the pressure would get to him if he had to think another two minutes.

Jim O'Brien kicked the ball from the 32-yard line. He made it. There were only four seconds left and the clock ran out on the following kickoff. That kick meant $15,000 dollars to each Colt player. And only $7,500 for each Dallas Cowboy. Tom Landry ran off the field just the same way he ran onto the field before the game. Stoically. To look at Landry then, you would never know how close a ball game that was. Or that he had lost. He's the same —win or lose. A helluva man.

On the morning of Super Bowl V, my crew met for breakfast at 8 o'clock Sunday morning at the Doral Hotel. We had gone over our mechanics and game plan the day before. We were free to enjoy breakfast. There would be no football during the meal.

We sat down and looked at the menu. I hadn't been in Miami all that season and I hadn't stayed previously at the Doral. Neither had any of the other men. We knew no one there.

The waitress came over, took all the orders but mine. When it was my turn to order, I was still undecided. I looked at the menu again and said, "I don't know whether to get ham and eggs or sausages and eggs."

The waitress didn't look up from her order book as she said, "That's probably the toughest call you'll make today."

I was caught by surprise. I thought no one knew me there. "Ham and eggs, please," I said quickly.

"Well, you blew that one," she said as she wrote down my order.

Hell, the game didn't start until one that afternoon. And I wasn't even wearing my uniform.

It's good to see Eddie LeBaron come back into the League as the general manager of the Atlanta Falcons. He was a great player without the size everyone says you have to have. Size and speed are two essentials in professional football, but nothing ever takes the place of intelligence. Eddie LeBaron is living proof of that. LeBaron had many outstanding years as a quarterback with the Redskins and Cowboys. He was the smallest man in the League the years he played, but only in size. When he fell back to throw, he would have to throw the ball almost straight up and out. When he didn't spot any eligible receivers, he would tuck that ball under his arm and run for yardage. It was quite a sight to see. Everyone had great respect for him. I did, for he never second-guessed an official. Something about Tom Landry rubs off on his players, especially those who are the leaders of the team.

I remember another hot Sunday in Dallas when everyone was a bit testy. The game was close and Cleveland was closing fast. One Cowboy player thought all the breaks were being given to the Cleveland team. Not Coach Landry though. He never said a word. According to this Dallas player, everything was wrong and nothing was right with the officiating. During a time-out, I ambled over to the Dallas team's huddle to tell them that they had only one more time-out left. This brought a few choice remarks from the chronic bitcher. "Hey, Ref, I bet you are even screwing us on the time-outs." It was not a question the way he said it.

I looked at him, pretended to be pissed off and suggested that I would take care of the time-outs and calls, although we appreciated his tremendous help. One of the Dallas players jokingly told me, "You had better be careful how you talk to him. He is our players' representative."

I turned to LeBaron and said, "Eddie, you're a lawyer during the off-season. How about taking my case?"

LeBaron grinned as he shook his head. "Sorry, I'm representing him. He can't lose the way you've been working today."

Tom Landry may not appear to be demonstrative, but he certainly is not dispassionate. He never tries to embarrass an official, though we probably have given him reasons to over the years. At least I must have. Landry never badgers, heckles, baits or bullies a referee. That's not his style. I'm not saying that heckling a referee is poor coaching. I am just saying that with an experienced professional referee, it means nothing and never gets the coach that fair advantage. Landry just doesn't do that. He might be disturbed and distressed at a penalty called against his team, but he won't tell you. Or hint it to the home crowd. I've never seen Coach Landry blow his top, rant, stomp or bite at a referee. He never has been hot-tempered, quick-tempered or short-tempered. All he has been is a winner.

Paul Brown

Paul Brown's record speaks for him: one hundred and sixty-six wins. Not only was Paul Brown a demanding coach of his players, he was equally as demanding of the officials. Paul Brown never swore. At least I never heard him. And I gave him ample opportunities with some of the calls that I made against his Cleveland Browns and Cincinnati Bengals. He was consistent in his attitudes over the years. As far as I am concerned, he never changed too much. He worked hard, and he insisted that the referee work as hard. If my call was in the questionable area (to him, not to me), he would invariably say, "It had better be in the films."

And if I was right, he'd tell me the next time he saw me. "You were right on that call in Pittsburgh." And if I was wrong, he really told me.

I remember a game in Washington one year. It's one that I can't forget. I imagine Paul Brown hasn't forgotten either. I never had a game like that before, or since. Cleveland was playing the Redskins. On Cleveland's first three plays, there were three consecutive major fouls. All against Cleveland. It was first and 55 yards to go for a first down for them. Later in the game with the score tied 10–10, Washington threw a forward pass 50 yards which fell incomplete in the end zone. No problem, right? Wait a minute. The field judge threw his flag for defensive pass interference in the end zone. That put the ball on Cleveland's one-yard line. A good but tough call. Washington tried twice to plunge the ball over. No luck. On third down they threw a short pass to the deep right-hand corner of the end zone. It was incomplete. But there was another flag on the play. Again against Cleveland. Defensive holding. That gave the Redskins the ball on Cleveland's half-yard line with first down. Four downs to get a half-yard. Washington finally pushed the ball over on fourth down, but barely. That meant Washington had needed seven downs to get one yard for a score. When they scored, Cleveland never did believe the man was over the goal line. But the head linesman's hands shot up for a touchdown.

With the score now 17–10 and the clock running down, Jim Brown of Cleveland broke across his right guard and went 80 yards for the tying touchdown. Wait a second. Was that another flag on the ground at the line of scrimmage? It sure was. Joe Muha, the umpire, had seen the guard grab and hold the defensive man long enough to spring Brown for his run. That was when he threw his flag. The place went wild. Especially when I walked off the penalty. Muha couldn't understand the noise. He glanced at the stands, shrugged his shoulders and said, "What's the noise for? Why the hell are they yelling? Didn't they ever see a holding call before?"

"Joe, it's been a rough afternoon for them. Penalty-wise. It gets them a little upset when their man runs eighty yards for the tying touchdown and you call it back."

"Did he score? No wonder they're mad. But Number Sixty-five held. Sprung Brown loose. Maybe he wouldn't have gone anywhere if the guard didn't hold and spring him." I nodded and kept walking off the 15 yards.

We weren't out of the woods yet. Cleveland finally went in for the tying touchdown. That made the score 17–16 for Washington. Lou Groza came in for his automatic extra-point try. He never missed. He didn't this time either. Wait another second. The head linesman had his flag down against Cleveland for offside. That wiped off the extra point and gave Cleveland another shot at it but from five yards farther back. Still a piece of cake for Groza. He never missed from that close. He kicked the ball and wham— the ball hits the crossbar and bounces back onto the field. No score or point. That left Washington the winner 17–16. I didn't even look back at Coach Brown. I got out of there real fast. The next day I read in the papers that Coach Brown said, "They should give the game ball to Schachter and his crew. They gained more yards than both teams combined."

Paul Brown was a master of the game. He was an intense person, fundamentally sound in every aspect of the game. He worked full blast at the job. He was a winner. I've never known a referee who didn't respect him highly.

Don Shula

Don Shula learned quite a bit from Paul Brown. As a player Shula was a cornerback for Coach Brown on the Cleveland team. He was then an assistant coach with Blanton Collier at the University of Kentucky. He moved to help George Wilson at Detroit and then took over the head coaching job at Baltimore. Collier had been Paul Brown's assistant for years, and he believed in Brown's philosophy of coaching.

It never failed. After every nationally televised game I refereed in Miami or another ball park, Shula and I always talked on the sideline sometime during the game. People thought he was chewing me out. And telling me off.

Coach Shula never told me off or chewed me out when I spoke to him on the sidelines during a time-out. He always inquired about my left Achilles tendon, which had ripped in a Minnesota-Baltimore game when he coached the Colts. The Vikings were playing the Colts in Minnesota one season when I was put out of action for one whole year. I was literally stepped on by a Minnesota tackle and *pop!*—there went my Achilles tendon. I thought that I had been shot. Or swatted by a 2-by-4.

Joe Kapp, then quarterback for the Vikings, took the snap and fell back to throw. He never made it. The defensive end of the Colts breezed right by the offensive tackle as if he weren't in the same ball park. The Colt player hit Kapp from the blind side, which caused a fumble. Another Colt player picked up the ball and ran for a touchdown.

The offensive tackle who had missed his block turned to follow the play. He ran right up my left leg and ripped my Achilles tendon off the bone into little bits and pieces and severed the tendon. It was a bang-bang play. And I was really banged. It took a year's therapy, 20 minutes swimming daily, seven miles of bicycle riding every day, leg weights, daily running, walking and lots of praying. I really worried when I worked the College All-Stars in Chicago the following season in my first game since the injury.

Funny thing about my Achilles play: the touchdown didn't count. Don Shinnick was the strong linebacker for the Colts. He was caught holding on that play, so the down didn't count and had to be replayed. No score and a five-yard penalty and an automatic first down for the Vikings. Imagine getting hit and being out for a year on a play that didn't even count. From that year on, any player wanting to hit me would have to chase me right up into the stands.

It's strange how misery loves company. That night after the game in which I ripped the Achilles tendon, I caught a Western Airlines flight out of Minneapolis to Los Angeles. In over two and a half million miles of flying, I've never had any plane trouble once we were airborne. With this one exception. An hour out of Minneapolis, the plane lost an engine and limped back to the airport. There I sat with my ankle in a bucket of ice, a worried look on my face, and the realization that I would face an operation the next day.

I finally reached home five hours late. My wife always picked me up. She didn't know that I had been knocked down and injured and that I couldn't walk. The airline provided a wheelchair which George Murphy, my head linesman, pushed. He had returned to Los Angeles with me. Just before my wife picked me up, she had run into another referee who had worked somewhere else in the east. He was an old friend. He was a gentleman, for he took her hand and kissed it and said, "Charlotte, it's so nice to see you again." Very chic and Continental, I guess. And very unlike him as a rule.

My wife thought, He must have had a couple of drinks on the plane back. I know he can't drink on the way to the game, so he must have had one or two with his dinner. Probably had a tough ball game.

When she spotted Murphy wheeling me out of the terminal,

she thought, Gosh, those two are drunk too. That's the kind of sympathy a football referee gets, even from his own wife. And there I sat with a ripped Achilles tendon. I didn't know which hurt more, my wife's attitude or my Achilles. But my Achilles was sure tender.

When I was in the hospital, I read the story of Thetis and her son Achilles. She took him and dipped him in the River Styx to make him invulnerable, but his heel in her hand remained dry. Achilles was then slain by an arrow wound in the heel, the one weak spot. And Achilles wasn't even a football referee.

The operation was successful. The next season I refereed one of my first League games in Baltimore. In the second quarter I moved back, stepped on some wet spot and *bang!* I felt a pop in my right calf. It scared me half to death. I thought it was the other Achilles tendon. I don't know if they ever had a nationally televised shot of a grown referee crying on the football field. If they had snapped me then, it would have been a first. I limped through the quarter and struggled back to the Colts' dressing room during half time. I lifted myself onto the training table. The team doctor looked at it. It was the plantaris muscle in my right calf. Not the Achilles, as I feared. It hurt for four weeks and then scarred over. Shula was also coach of the Colts that season.

That's what we talked about on the sideline. Coach Shula would always ask, "How's your tendon? Bother you any? Looks like you move okay. Not too fast. But then you never did move too fast."

John Unitas also severed his Achilles tendon. We used to discuss tendons out on the field. I'm sure people thought we were talking football. Or that he was annoyed about a call. We never did exchange X rays though.

I was in Miami the year after Joe Namath and the New York Jets shocked the football world by beating Baltimore in Super Bowl III. I had just finished refereeing a Miami-Jets game. I don't even remember the score, or who won. But I do remember getting scared to death.

I was sitting in the Miami airport, waiting to board the plane to Los Angeles. As I was talking to Jack Fette in the lounge, I heard blood-curdling yelps coming straight toward me. It was a crowd of women, about thirty to forty of them, running down the corridor. I knew it had been a tough ball game, but nothing had happened that would bring the wolves after me. I quickly got up, stepped behind a post and tried to hide. Then I saw what they were chasing. It was Joe Namath. He was about five yards or so ahead of them. He was moving pretty good for Namath. Joe had those bad legs, and didn't maneuver too quickly. But he was quick then.

Joe Namath was at the height of his career. And it was a well-deserved career. But his legs and knees were always a problem. That day he moved like Jesse Owens did in his prime. He stayed ahead of the pack. It was a mixed bunch of girls, middle-aged women and some senior citizens. They were gaining on him. Namath neared the departure gate. He ran quickly toward the Jets' charter plane and boarded it. They slammed the doors shut and taxied away. His teammates were already on the plane, waiting for him.

I had never seen such adulation by a group for an athlete before. Not for Unitas, Starr, Jim Brown, Frank Gifford, Lombardi, or even for O. J. Simpson later on. It was unbelievable. The women hung around the departure gate, letting off their pent-up emotions. I wasn't about to take any chances. What if someone spotted me? It could become a case of love turned to hate within a few seconds. I headed straight for the nearest men's room—and almost missed my plane.

I had Miami on the road one Sunday afternoon. It was their last game prior to the play-off time. The Dolphins had won the Super Bowl the previous year and were in the money again. Before the game, Coach Shula saw me. "Norm, we're hurting. I mean physically. We are short four players. Tell your crew not to throw any of our guys out. We need everybody we have all afternoon."

I nodded my head. It didn't matter if I nodded or not. We don't throw anybody for the throwing. We never run them unless it is an extreme violation. Just after the game started, one of the Miami defensive players, #79, ran after one of the offensive blockers. He was mad. Furious. It looked as if he would kill him. He threw a forearm which missed by two feet as he saw me. Close only counts in horseshoes.

This happened near the Miami bench. I yelled at the player. Before I could say anything, Shula yelled, "Remember. We're short four players today. Don't run any of them."

I glanced at Coach Shula and said, "Tell Number Seventy-nine to watch himself. He's going to take himself out of there if he hits someone. It'll be a fast shower."

Shula nodded. When I looked back, he was talking to #79 pretty good. Would you believe that #79 walked by me and said he was sorry. He was with us all game. That's why I call Coach Shula a real pro.

In 1972, when Don Shula's team, the Miami Dolphins, won 14 consecutive League games, it was a first not only for Shula, but for any team since 1932. The Pittsburgh Steelers did the same thing in 1978. Miami's first play-off game after their undefeated 14-game season was with Buffalo. I was the referee of the game. Mel Hein, the former Hall of Fame center of the New York Giants and then the assistant supervisor of the NFL officials, was in town to be the League observer in the press box for the game. The NFL has a League observer at every game. The observer doesn't over-rule the referee, but acts as the eyes and ears for the League in case any problems arise at the game. The observer's job is to pass on pertinent professional information on how the officials have worked, and what plays the League film reviewers should scrutinize in their film reviews. All games are reviewed.

Mel Hein and I were sitting in my room at the Doral Hotel in Miami on Saturday the day before the Miami-Buffalo game. We were watching the other first-round divisional play-off between Oakland and Pittsburgh. It was a tough game. It looked like it was all over. Oakland led by a score of 7–6. The Steelers had the ball on fourth down with less than 25 seconds left in the game. And still 60 yards to go for a score. Too far for a possible winning field goal.

Terry Bradshaw, the Steelers' quarterback, spotted his running back Frenchy Fuqua downfield. He threw him the ball. Just as Fuqua went up for the pass, Jack Tatum, the hard-rocking and -socking defensive back of Oakland, also jumped up for the ball at the same time. The pass went off Fuqua's fingers and fell toward the ground. The game looked over.

Franco Harris came up with the now famous "Immaculate Reception." He caught the ball at his shoe tops and kept running. All the way for a touchdown and the winning score. On the last play of the game.

All hell broke loose. Coach Madden and all the Raiders screamed, "Illegal catch. Double touch. Score doesn't count."

At that time the rule stated, "No offensive player may catch the ball unless a defensive player touched the ball prior to the second touching by the offense." The rule was changed in 1978 to legalize the double touch.

Did Jack Tatum touch the ball before Harris' catch? The stadium was rocking, for the game was being played in Pittsburgh. The players milled all over the field and the referee ran to the field phone. He called upstairs. To the press box. That's where Art McNally, the League observer, was watching the game. With a television set.

After a few seconds' conversation, the referee ran back to the field and signaled touchdown. McNally didn't make the call. The official on the play did. He saw the ball touch Tatum's shoulder before Franco Harris caught it. Legal all the way. Coach Madden never believed the call. But it was a good call. One of the closest calls possible.

Mel Hein and I watched the entire confusion on the field. No referee likes to see another referee get involved. I felt for him. Hein looked over at me, looked back to the television screen, and heard the announcer say, "The referee is checking with McNally in the press box."

Finally, Hein spoke. "Norm, you promise not to call me in the press box tomorrow if something happens in the Miami-Buffalo game, don't you?"

Fortunately, our game the next day was an easy one. Shula's team was too strong. And O. J. Simpson couldn't get untracked for the Buffalo Bills that afternoon. After Miami had scored several times and was in complete control of the game, Lou Saban, Buffalo's coach and now the president of the New York Yankees baseball team, called me over during a time-out.

"Norm, I know it's a one-sided game. But let's have the officials call the fouls out there. Forget the score and work the game."

Maybe we were getting careless, but I still don't believe it. We work the game, not the score.

The second-touch play was always a pain in the ass. Never

clean-cut. Occasionally, a pass would go off a receiver's hands, bounce up into the air, and another offensive receiver downfield would catch it. Wide-open play. No strain, no pain. Easy call. Illegal catch.

But it never seemed to work that way. Especially not for me in Super Bowl V. That was the game between the Dallas Cowboys and Baltimore in Miami. In the second quarter one of those so-called double touches happened. A most pivotal call. A close call. One that has been rehashed a thousand times. The Dallas players still don't believe it. They couldn't believe many things that occurred in that ball game. Some writers dubbed that Super Bowl game the "Blooper Bowl."

One of the two most controversial calls that day was another of "Was it or wasn't it? a double touch?" Johnny Unitas, of the Colts, threw a pass to his receiver, Ed Hinton. The ball went off his hands and over the defensive back Mel Renfro's head. Or did it? John Mackey, the powerful tight end of the Colts, caught the ball and scored. The play was good for a 75-yard touchdown.

I saw the jumping action of Hinton and Tatum back where I was standing with Johnny Unitas. I didn't know if Mel Renfro had touched the ball or not. I knew it was close and I had better double-check to see if it was a touchdown. It would have been too late to check at half time. So down I ran to the back judge who had been right on the play. I wasn't going to signal touchdown until I checked. Better late than sorry.

I ran downfield to chat with the back judge. On my way downfield I ran by Ed Marion, the head linesman. "Ed, did you get a good look at that play? Did Renfro touch the ball?"

Marion gave me the "I didn't see a thing" gesture. That told me it was really close. I finally got to the back judge. "Did Renfro touch that ball?"

"I think he did."

"You got to be sure. Are you sure?"

"I'm sure that I think he did."

That was good enough for me. He had been right on the play, knew the rule and ruled correctly. That's why they pay him.

The following day NFL films showed the play in slow motion. They showed that the ball continued to spiral after going off Hinton's hand in the direction of Renfro's outstretched fingers and into the hands of Mackey. Fortunately, there was a good picture of the ball spiraling as it passed Renfro, and then flopping over. Somebody had to touch the ball to change its spin. The only thing there was Renfro's hand. That's what it touched. Close call, but a good call. Chalk one for our side.

The other controversial call in that ball game was Jack Fette's decision on a fumble at the Colts' two-yard line. It was another bang-bang call. Fette was right on the play. Dallas still thinks he missed it. A couple of years later our crew was in Dallas for a ball game. In a Dallas paper the day of the game, a reporter reminded his readers that "Norm Schachter's crew is in town. That means Jack Fette is the line judge." It went on to say several other things.

On the opening kickoff of that game, Ike Thomas, of Dallas, caught the ball in the end zone and ran 101 yards for a touchdown. The place was wild. Before I signaled touchdown, I ran over to Fette.

"Jack, you don't have a flag on this play, do you?"

"No. Why?"

"Just checking. If you did, neither one of us would get out of here alive. It would be murder, if you had your flag down for a clip or something. Imagine if you had called that one back. They would shoot both of us."

If there had been a clip, Fette's flag would have dropped. Nothing intimidates him. That's why he is in the League. I always referred to Marion and Fette as "my bookends." They certainly hold down the sidelines.

Two years after the controversial double-touch play in Super Bowl V, I was in San Diego to give the Chargers a rules talk before the season opened. Johnny Unitas, who had been the quarterback for the Colts that game, and Pettis Norman, a receiver from Dallas in the Super Bowl V, were now teammates on the San Diego team. They were sitting next to each other when I got up to give the rules talk.

Before I could start, Pettis Norman piped up, "Norm, you still owe me seven thousand five hundred dollars. Renfro never touched that ball."

Winners of the Super Bowl received $15,000. Losers got $7,500. Pettis Norman wanted that $7,500 difference. I looked at him. Then looked at Unitas, who was on his left. "I don't owe it to you. I didn't get the money. I get the same fee no matter who wins.

Unitas got a winning share. He's right next to you. Why doesn't he give it to you?"

Unitas put his hand in his pocket, took out his money clip and turned toward Pettis Norman. "Pettis, how much did you say it was?"

Coach Don Shula has changed over the years. I remember when he was an assistant coach. And then when he became the head man of the Baltimore Colts. Then head coach of the Miami Dolphins. At the beginning he had been a highly emotional coach. Shula has mellowed over the years. He still has that sharp needle and a great sense of humor. He used to prowl the sidelines but in the last half-dozen years or so, he'd needle for that fair advantage from a standing position. He was a hollerer, still is at times. He has my respect, is one of my favorites and is a winner. His victory record is close to 200 wins and still going up. That record isn't what places him high on my list. It is his understanding and appreciation that the officials are pros and they also have a tough job.

Remember when I said that Joe Kapp was hit from the blind side in the game in which I had ripped my Achilles tendon? Being hit from the blind side means someone blocks, belts or bowls you over from the side you're not looking at. You are looking in the other direction and can't and don't see the other fellow hit you. Nothing funny about getting hit, but let me tell what happened one day in Philadelphia years ago with Les Richter. Richter later became president of Riverside International Race Track. A real success story.

Richter was tough. He hit and got hit. Opposing players kept an eye on him before, during and after a play. They wanted to know where he was at all times. I liked him. He had a great sense of humor. He needled all the time. He played hard, and took as much as he handed out. And he never bitched about the officiating. At least not any more than most players.

That one time in Philadelphia, Richter was all over Van Brocklin, a former teammate of his on the Rams. Bob Pellegrini was the middle linebacker of the Eagles then. He chased Richter after that game. They exchanged more than mere words. It was after the game, so the players were on their own time. It surprised me, for Pellegrini had a sense of humor. He always referred to me as Bert Bell's henchman.

It's funny what you remember about a player. Richter was a helluva player, but yet I remember him best for what he said to me that interesting afternoon in Philadelphia. Van Brocklin had handed off the ball and I followed the play. I reached in too fast to get the ball after the tackle was made, and was accidentally knocked off my feet from the side. I was more startled than stunned. Richter reached over to help me up and asked, "You okay? What happened?"

I felt foolish, embarrassed, and answered, "I must have been hit from the blind side."

"Yeah," Richter said, "right between the eyes."

Coaches Who
Made Me Laugh

No one will disagree with me when I say there are other excellent coaches in the League. Some are just luckier than others. Some are better than others. I remember a rules talk in Oakland one year. Coach Madden and his players were a bit upset because one official had called pass interference against them the week before. They couldn't understand it, for another official hadn't called a foul on a similar play the week before that.

"Say, Norm. How come one official will call it one way and another official will call it another way? How come one guy is better than the other guy?"

I didn't even ask which official was better. I didn't have to. I looked at Coach Madden and the players and answered, "You guys surprise me. How come there are better players than others? This may come as a shock to some of you, but there are some coaches who are better than other coaches. Whenever you have two people doing the same thing, one is going to be better. We want all officials to be consistent in their calls. We just try to keep the differences very small. But when it comes to ability, judgment, guts or experience—hell, they're all different. Why you accept the differences in ballplayers but not in officials kills me. This may come as a surprise to all of you, but officials are just like people."

I am not trying to say that there were only six top coaches in the League. I just listed my top choices. There have been and still are other excellent coaches in the National Football League, coaches like Ewbank, Allen, Noll, Grant, Gillman, Stram and my own personal favorite, Norm Van Brocklin. I remember coaches more from what they said to me out on the field than from their win-loss record. I recall things coaches said to me over the years, especially when they handed me a laugh. I looked for that laugh while watching to make sure no one got that fair advantage.

Take Weeb Ewbank. He coached both an NFL team and an AFL team to championships. He won over 130 games and that's a lot of games. A great record. He was a feisty coach. I particularly remember him. Ewbank was the first one I ever heard say to me, "I don't want any breaks. Just give me my fair advantage."

In the over 400 professional football games that I have refereed, I have seen hundreds of coaches come and go. They differ in size, philosophy, personality and ability. They all feel the same way about getting their fair advantage. That's what makes my job as a referee so much fun.

Weeb Ewbank was always looking for that advantage. I think back, and I can well remember a tough Bear-Colt game in noisy Baltimore. The gun had ended the first half, and we all were running off the field as it was a bit nippy in Baltimore that day. The score was 21–7 in favor of the Bears so you know that Ewbank wasn't getting his share of the fair advantage. As I ran by Ewbank, he looked at me and told me, "They scored once on us and twice on you." And I wasn't even playing.

It's funny the things a referee remembers about a coach. I can remember another day in Baltimore when Green Bay and the Colts were having a donnybrook. That means all hell was breaking loose. Nothing seemed to go right. There were days like that. Fortunately, not too many, or else I would have been long gone before my 22 years in the League.

One of the Colt players had come in hard and really belted Bart Starr after he had released the ball. There was no doubt in my mind. I called it then and I would call it the same way now. No question about it. It was an open-and-shut case of roughing the passer. I threw my flag. It kept the Packers' drive alive. Paul Hornung went in and scored soon after. It was the ball game. At least that's what Coach Ewbank said. And how he said it!

It was after the game that Weeb Ewbank came into our dressing room. I was showering but I heard him say, "Where's Norm?" The other officials told him I was in the showers. He said, "I'll wait for him." That's what he thought.

I stayed in the showers twenty minutes until he called it a day. I was the cleanest man in Baltimore that day. As Ewbank left, he shouted, "Norm, you'll never wash the smell out of your last call no matter how long you shower."

It will come as a surprise to many, especially Coach Van Brocklin, but I enjoyed him more than any other coach over the years. He was always mad, said nasty things, never complimented me (or any other official), swore, but oh—what a great sense of humor. He was the first coach of the Minnesota Vikings and they were tough years. Especially one game I refereed in Green Bay. The Packers versus the Vikings.

Green Bay was on its way to another championship. They needed to win. The Vikings were going no place, but they also needed a win. Over anybody. Especially over Green Bay. The score of the game was 24–19, in favor of Green Bay, in the last 40 seconds when Fran Tarkenton dropped back and threw a 40-yard touchdown pass to "Red" Phillips. Wait a minute. There flew a penalty flag. Art Holst, the back judge, who was in his first year and who was doing a great job, had spotted offensive pass interference. That made no touchdown and a 15-yard penalty against Minnesota. Van Brocklin was speechless, but he was making sounds. Like dirty words. There were still 30 seconds left to play. Tarkenton dropped back again and threw a long, long pass. Bill Brown, #30, caught the ball in the end zone. Art Holst watched Brown's feet and noticed that Brown's second step touched the end line. Not a completed pass in the NFL, as both feet of the receiver have to land in bounds. That's unlike the college rule, which requires only one foot to be in bounds. Holst signaled "no good" immediately. Brown was wild. He chased Holst and pushed him. There came the flag again. And here came Holst up to me. I was standing in the middle of the field. Everyone was screaming. Van Brocklin had to be restrained and I was pissed off.

I looked at Holst. I didn't want that kind of help. I looked again at Holst, knew he was a new official and a good one. He had been right on both calls and had been in great position in both calls. He was uptight. I needed to relax him.

"Holst," I said. "Take one step backward. You're spitting in my face."

There we were on national television. Holst with the biggest call in his life and I'm telling him he's spitting in my face.

"What, what?" he said. "I'm ejecting Number Thirty for pushing me."

"Holst, when you say you're ejecting Number Thirty, you mean you're running his ass off the field. Right?"

"Right."

"That may be right for you. I have to go over to The Dutchman and tell him that Number Thirty is out of the game. And you just took two touchdowns away from him. You know, there aren't too many officials in the country who even get to work one year in the NFL."

I walked toward the Minnesota bench. Van Brocklin's mouth was going a mile a minute. I didn't hear a word, but I knew every word he called me. I didn't get closer than 10 yards from the sideline and yelled over, "Coach, Number Thirty is out of the game."

He yelled back. I'm not sure what, but he yelled. And yelled.

I started the game again. Just before the snap of the ball, Holst blew his whistle and came running up to me. His position was on the sideline with the Vikings close to him. When he got close, he told me, "I'm going to throw my flag on the Minnesota bench. The players and Van Brocklin are calling me every dirty name in the book."

I stared at Holst. "Art," I told him, and tried to keep my voice down, "if you throw that flag, I'm going to personally come down to your position, pick up your flag, and shove it up your ass. Don't throw your flag. We've taken two touchdowns away from them, penalized them thirty yards, ran Brown out of the game and you're telling me they're swearing at you. Hell, they should shoot you."

Holst didn't bat an eye. He had guts and his calls were right. "Norm, they're swearing at me. I can hear them."

"Art, if you can hear them from where you stand, get the hell over to the other side of the field. We've got eight seconds left, so let's get out of here alive. Move away from their side of the field. And keep that damn flag in your pocket."

We got the play in. The gun went off. I ran like hell. I looked back and there was Holst running, and Van Brocklin and most of the Minnesota players were running too. Right behind Holst. And gaining. I reached the dressing room, jumped inside and closed the door fast. Within two seconds Holst was pounding on the door. "Let me in, let me in, Norm."

I opened the door and in he came. As we all sat quietly, I said, "You know, fellows, next year someplace someone along the road will ask, 'Say, what was the name of that official who made those calls at Minnesota?' "

Art Holst is still working as an official. Damn good too. Has had several Super Bowl assignments. He was correct on his calls then, and he still is. And he's probably one of the very best after-dinner speakers in the country. Hell, he should be. A lot has happened to him.

I received a call from the Commissioner's office the Tuesday following that Green Bay-Minnesota game. The Commissioner fines disqualified players as a rule. Especially if they push an official. The Commissioner had fined Brown, but Van Brocklin said that he never had been notified personally by the referee (me) that Brown had been removed from the game. That is a must. The League office then called me to check whether I had notified Van Brocklin about the disqualification of Brown.

"Norm, did you tell Van Brocklin that Brown was out of the game? He claims that he never heard you tell him that."

I didn't even think for a minute. "I'm sure, I'm sure. I told him; I'm also sure that he never heard me. He wasn't listening to what I said. He was telling me what to do. I didn't hear him either. Maybe I should have gone up to him and discussed it. No way. I just yelled it from ten to fifteen yards out from the sideline."

Van Brocklin had a way with words. Who else would you ever hear say "Your asshole sucks canal water?" He never beat around the bush.

When the fans, sports writers and TV commentators questioned the ease with which field goals were kicked and ball games were won and wondered what could be done about it, the League finally moved the goalposts back 10 yards to the end line and brought all unsuccessful field goal attempts back to the previous spot (center snap spot). Now when the kick is over 30 yards, the coach has to decide whether to chance a field goal or whether he should punt the ball. Most of the field goal kickers were players from Europe, soccer-type kickers. Sidewinders, we called them. Van Brocklin didn't think there was a problem regarding the field goal and what to do. When asked, he said, "No problem. All they've got to do is to tighten the immigration laws."

Coach Van Brocklin and my line judge, Jack Fette, didn't see eye to eye too often. Too often is like never. Every time Van Brocklin swore at Fette, Fette would swear back, like a couple of kids. One day in Atlanta, Van Brocklin was furious at Fette. At the two-minute warning I went over to Van Brocklin to notify him. Fette was standing close by. Instead of talking to Fette, Van Brocklin told me, "Tell your fat, fuckin' friend Fette he's screwing me again."

Fette heard all of it, but kept his eyes riveted on the field. I looked over at Fette, turned to Van Brocklin and answered, "Coach, I just work with him. He's no fuckin' friend of mine."

Super Bowl One was played in Los Angeles. I was the referee of that game. Art McNally, presently the Supervisor of Officials in the NFL, worked it also. The Super Bowl headquarters was at the Los Angeles Hilton Hotel. Art and I went for lunch in the coffee shop the day before the game. As we walked into the coffee shop, Van Brocklin was sitting at a table with a fellow coach. Art and I walked in that direction as there was an empty table close by. As we reached the table, Van Brocklin looked up and said, "You blind clowns were probably sent to this game to see how a game should be worked. They couldn't have assigned you two to this kind of a game. You are probably here for the experience."

Once in New York City our crew was to work a Giants-Vikings game. We went to Toots Shor's place for dinner. Many of the sports people ate there, it served good food and we were big eaters. Herm Rohrig, Adrian Burk, Joe Connell, Burl Toler and I walked into Toots's eatery. Toots was with Van Brocklin at his table. When he saw our crew, Toots turned to Van Brocklin, said something and pointed at us. Van Brocklin got up in his seat, pointed his finger at us and yelled, "You robbers." And sat down.

I liked Van Brocklin. You always knew where you stood with him. Always in the same place. He was my kind of a coach: a great sense of humor, and always good for a laugh or two a ball game. But you paid for it.

And Other Coaches with a Sense of Humor

Buddy Parker had 14 years as a head coach in the NFL, six of them as head man at Detroit and eight more at Pittsburgh. Not that many years ago either. But I remember him well. Especially the way he told me what he thought of me.

Parker had a dry sense of humor. He had been around long enough to know what the score was when it came to rules and signals. In a ball game in Pittsburgh one day, Parker's fullback was having a tough time. Every time he was tackled, he let the ball roll forward out of his hands. It rolled forward a few feet each time. Sometimes he actually threw the ball forward after he was downed. I had to go get the ball. I told him to knock it off.

"Number Thirty-five, don't throw the ball forward when you're tackled. Let it stay right where you are. I don't want to chase that damn ball."

Number 35 looked at me. He nodded. He knew what I was saying. The next time he carried the ball, he was tackled after a five-yard gain. It was close to a first down. Just before #35 was going to let go of the ball, I yelled, "Number Thirty-five, don't throw that ball."

Something must have bugged #35. Maybe it was the way I had yelled. He threw the ball at me and said, "Here, you sonavabitch."

That didn't bother me. I measured off 15 yards for unsportsmanlike conduct and gave the signal.

At the end of the half, Coach Parker was waiting for me. "Say, what was the unsportsmanlike conduct foul for?"

I told him, "Number Thirty-five threw the ball at me and called me a sonavabitch."

Parker looked at me and said, "You're right. He shouldn't have thrown the ball at you."

Some referees must rub coaches the wrong way. Some coaches use referees as an escape hatch for their lack of ability, wrongdoings or mishandling of personnel. Very seldom do we see a coach who constantly blames the referee. We know many players who never foul. At least that's what they say and believe. When a penalty flag is thrown against these players, they get that hurt, bewildered look in their eyes which speaks for them. You know what I mean. "Foul? Me? Never. I didn't touch him. How could you call that? I never foul anyone."

Bullshit.

Some coaches stay just long enough to have a cup of coffee in the National Football League. They are in and out of the League so quickly that a referee doesn't really get to know their names. It is a revolving-door concept. Here today, gone tomorrow.

Houston had one of those a number of years ago. His team never lost. The referee stole it from him, the players didn't put out, and the press was against him. That's the song he sang.

I was in the Astrodome one Sunday afternoon. It was raining outside but it was warm and cozy inside the Dome. A perfectly delightful way to officiate a ball game in adverse weather conditions. Houston was losing again, and the coach didn't understand it. Again. One of his defensive players had just run into the kicker and bowled him over. It was the easiest call I had had all season long. Cut and dried. I threw my flag, measured off the yardage and was about to give the ready-to-play signal when the Houston team called time out. The coach wanted to speak to me. I walked over to the Houston bench.

The coach was furious. He shouted, "You're the worst referee in the entire National Football League."

I looked at him and said, "You may be right, Coach. But wouldn't that be a most unusual coincidence?"

✷   ✷   ✷

Assistant coaches reflect their head coach. If he is a screamer, the assistants will scream. If the head coach is quiet, the assistants will be quiet. They key off the head man. I think back to Vince Lombardi. He didn't swear. His assistant coaches didn't swear. If anyone was going to scream at a referee from the Green Bay side, it would be Lombardi. He didn't allow anyone else to badger the referee. That was his job. He knew how to do it. He didn't need any help.

Millions of television watchers have the wrong impression. Maybe they get it from some old ballplayer. Maybe they like to think the language out on the field is dirty and obscene. Far from it. Oh, there are lots of times players forget and are angry. Especially when they feel they have been fouled. And it wasn't called. They will swear then. Never at a referee, especially a referee who has been around for a number of years. Coaches and players realize that it is an automatic penalty, especially if it is personal against the referee. It's tough enough to make yardage, let alone lose it through some careless talk. I only remember a couple of times when some coach or player swore at me. Never did it more than once. You can bet your life on that.

A couple of seasons ago an assistant coach who is no longer in the League became excited about a call by one of the officials. He yelled at me as I was walking off the penalty, "Hey, Ref, you stupid bastard."

Before the last word was out, my flag was down and I marched off an extra 15 for unsportsmanlike conduct. The last step took me close to his bench, so I turned to him and said, "Coach, don't you ever call me stupid."

In the last number of years Coach Bud Grant of the Vikings has become more expressive. And explosive. For years he had been the same. Stony-faced, unruffled and impassive. Always looked the same. I have never seen him smile in all the years he has been with the Minnesota Vikings. At least not on the field. He always looks stoical and grim.

I had a touch-and-go game one day in Minnesota. It was the fourth quarter, late in the game, and Minnesota was having its problems. The 49ers were getting close enough for a field goal. That would have been enough for a win. It was third down and

the 49ers ran the ball toward the center of the field so they could
eat up the clock and get better field position for the field goal.

Yup, you guessed it. The 49ers fumbled, and fumbled the game
away. Carl Eller, of Minnesota, recovered the ball and the game
was over as far as the 49ers were concerned. The Vikings ran out
the clock on the next two plays. As we were running to the dressing room, I looked over at Coach Bud Grant. I thought he would
be excited and smiling at the surprise and fortunate ending. He
still had the same grim look he always had, even after the lucky
win. I turned to Jim Marshall and asked, "I never saw Coach
Grant smile. Is he ever in a good mood? Does he ever smile?"

Marshall had a twinkle in his eyes and said, "I can't honestly
answer that. You see, I only have known him since 1967, the year
he took the job. That was only eight years ago."

Contrary to what people think, coaches are friends with referees. I won't say, "Some of my best friends are coaches," but I will
say that we are friends. The coaches have a job to do, and I have
a job to do. They continually look for that fair advantage, and I
try to see that no one gets it. I believe some of the coaches become better friends after they are released or they quit. Though I
don't know too many of them who have quit. They had a little
help along the way. Like by the owner or general manager who is
catching heat.

Let me tell you about a former head coach of the San Francisco
49ers who had a helluva sense of humor. Red Hickey, that's who.
He didn't take himself too seriously when he was head coach. He
was always good for a laugh an afternoon. And if his team was
ahead, then it was a couple of laughs that day. Hickey still has
that sense of humor today. I see him every so often around the
circuit when I hit the different cities. I like him. He knows how to
laugh. His needle kept me on my toes.

Red is now a scout for the Dallas Cowboys. I remember his first
year as head coach of the San Francisco 49ers. It had nothing to
do with his team or his coaching ability, but what he said one afternoon in the old Briggs Stadium, Detroit.

The Friday prior to the Sunday game in Detroit, I was involved
in a 15-car smashup on the freeway. It was an accordion type of
accident. One car came to a sudden stop and the rest of the 14

cars banged into one another. I was taken to the hospital for treatment. Though no bones were broken, I was pretty well cut up. I had 10 stitches in my bottom lip as it had been ripped open from one end to the other. I had hit the steering wheel. I looked and felt as though I had been in a cement mixer. TV and radio announcers in my area announced that I had been involved in a car accident and had been taken to the hospital. And hurt. My phone rang off the hook. People I hadn't heard from in 20 years called and wondered if I was still alive. And why. I hadn't realized that referees had such a spot in some people's hearts. I had to get out of town to get some rest. No better place than out on the field, refereeing a football game in Detroit. My doctor gave me a clearance to work the game so I flew out to Detroit. I looked awful. My eyes were black and blue, my lip had the thread of the stitches sticking out and my face was cut.

When I walked out on the field and walked over to both coaches, Hickey, of the 49ers, and George Wilson, of the Detroit Lions, I figured I would get some sympathy. I would milk all I could get from those two. As I approached both coaches, they looked at my swollen face, the stitches, my blackened eyes and the cuts all over my face. My appearance was not that of the All-American boy.

Hickey took a hard look at me. He then asked, "Where did you make you last call, Norm?"

That was the last kind word I had all afternoon. I never put the whistle to my mouth. I never blew a whistle. And I didn't throw a flag. I just went through the ball game. It worked out as well as any that I have had. I know that the players thought that I was the Hollywood type when they saw me at the airport after the game, drinking a beer through a straw and eating the strained baby food that I had brought along.

When I think of former great players who became head coaches, I can't help but think of Abe Gibron. I remember him well. He had been one of George Halas' assistant coaches at Chicago for years. Any afternoon in Chicago in those days was memorable. Anytime you're called a sonavabitch, it's memorable. And there were many memorable days in Chicago. Halas and his henchmen—everyone was in the act. The star attraction, of course, was Halas. His supporting cast was his assistants. My,

were they vocal! Gibron, Phil Handler and the others were priceless. Never speechless. Just priceless. They had the needle out all
the time. They kept all the referees on their toes. No daydreaming
for a referee any Sunday afternoon in Wrigley Field.

Abe Gibron, now the chief assistant coach for the Tampa Bay
Buccaneers, was head coach of the Chicago Bears at the time. Abe
was a great player. He never stopped coming. In fact, this time in
New Orleans he really kept coming. Right at me. Before I tell you
why, let me set up the preceding play that caused my words with
Gibron.

The Bears were in New Orleans. New Orleans had the ball on
Chicago's 12-yard line with 22 seconds remaining in the first half.
The Saints had one time-out remaining. It was fourth down. No
other choice but a field goal attempt. But not with 22 seconds left.
That would give the ball back to the Bears if the goal was good or
no good. With their two remaining time-outs left, the Bears would
then have a chance to score. This is where smarts count.

Archie Manning told me to stand by him. He would tell me
when he wanted the time out. That would stop the clock. Dick
Butkus, defensive captain of the Bears, stayed right with us.
There we were, the friendly three—Manning, the referee (me)
and Butkus—away from the others. We watched the clock run
down.

As the seconds ticked off, I watched Manning, the quarterback
and captain of the Saints. No way would I be responsible for the
clock running out without a play being had. Manning waited until
there were five seconds showing on the stadium clock. That would
have been just about right. It would have allowed New Orleans to
kick the field goal and end the half. Smart thinking. Par for the
course, though, in this type of a situation. It happens all the time.
But I never like it, for it puts the referee on spot to hear the "Time
out" call.

Just as Manning turned to me, Butkus said in a quiet voice,
which was out of character for him, "Say, Archie, you didn't get
hurt on that last play, did you? I saw you grab your shoulder."

Manning answered him, "No, I didn't." He then realized what
Butkus was doing. He had been set up. Manning yelled, "Time
out, Norm."

There was one second left. Butkus had almost had him. One
more sentence and good-bye field goal chance. The clock would

have run out. Butkus looked at me, shrugged his shoulders and said,"It almost worked."

Yes, it almost did work. If it had worked, I would have had a problem. Do you think anyone would have believed me if I had claimed that Manning had never called a time-out? I could see the papers in New Orleans the next day. In big letters, "REFEREE BLOWS ANOTHER." And wouldn't it have made a wonderful shot for Monday night television half time? I can see the picture. The three of us standing and looking up at the clock. Maybe a little music in the background with the old favorite "Three Blind Mice." Or one big rat.

After New Orleans' time out, I gave the ready-to-play signal. Both teams took their positions. But we weren't through yet. The Bears turned to Gerry Hart, my umpire, and called a time-out. Hart, unthinkingly, allowed it. Chicago wanted the place-kicker to have more time to get nervous, thinking about the field goal kick. I jumped in quickly and waved the time-out off. Consecutive time-outs are against the rules. New Orleans went ahead and kicked. Missed it too.

The half ended with the missed field goal. I turned to get the respective captains to find out which way the Bears wanted to receive. Before I could signal and yell for the captains, Abe Gibron was storming out to the center of the field, closely followed by his assistant coach, Jim Carr. It was quite a sight. Abe is a big man. Fast for his size too. He reached me in no time at all. He was wild. They had had only 10 men on the field when they had requested their time out. I didn't know that. It wouldn't have mattered. I was just interested in no one having more than 11 men on the field at one time. There is a difference.

Gibron and his assistant, Carr, met me at the center of the field. I wasn't too sure whether they had run out to meet me or get me. I didn't know which. Gibron got close to me and yelled, "Why didn't you give us a time-out?"

Carr was like an echo. "Why didn't you give me a time-out?" He didn't even say "us."

I finally got a word in. "Coach, let me answer your question. It's a rule. You can't have consecutive time-outs."

Coach Gibron was furious. "What kind of a rule is it? I only had ten men on the field."

I didn't even explain that the Rules Committee didn't even

think of 10 men when they passed the rule. Anyway, I told Gibron, "It's a rule. It's in the rule book."

Gibron turned to me and shouted, "I read the rule book."

Without thinking I said, "What color is it?"

Abe Gibron may not have known what color the rule book was, but his face was turning all colors. I got the hell out of there real fast.

The last couple of seasons Abe Gibron coached the Chicago Bears were lean ones. Very lean. That means the team didn't win too often. Or not often enough. That's when fans get vocal. There's really nothing a head coach can do if he doesn't have the horses. He needs the material. Some coaches can get more from some players than others. But if a team is short certain skill positions, it's not going anywhere. Chicago was short those players during Gibron's tenure. Gibron knew his stuff and was a fine coach.

At game time one Sunday afternoon there were signs all over Soldier Field in Chicago. None were complimentary toward the head coach. Fans wanted him out. Gone. Some signs and placards were funny, some downright insulting and some crude. It had to bug Gibron. I even was mad at the fans, for Gibron was good and a damn fair person. I know the fans pay for their tickets, but viciousness is something else. The payoff came when a helicopter flew above the stadium with a sign, "I PREDICT YOU WILL LOSE AGAIN TODAY, COACH GIBRON."

I was at the sidelines giving Coach Gibron the two-minute warning for the first half. He didn't hear me. He kept looking at that damn helicopter. He finally turned toward me and said to one of his assistants, "Get the number of that plane. We'll report it. Or let's shoot it down."

I didn't blame Coach Gibron a bit, and his team did lose that day.

When I speak of signs at stadiums, I can't help but think back to Yankee Stadium and Allie Sherman. He was the New York Giants coach for eight years and won over fifty ball games. His teams were always in contention and near the top of the League every year. During his last few years as coach in New York, there were "GOOD-BYE ALLIE" signs all over the stadium. And the fans kept screaming it every time he stepped out on the field. I didn't like to see that, but as a referee I didn't mind. Every time they go after a coach, they leave the referee alone. No, I was not responsible for the signs. But it had crossed my mind at times in other stadiums.

I remember Coach Sherman well. He was a good coach. Had quite a number of successful seasons. Then the players got older, lost a step or two, and the close games they always won then became losses. That's the way it goes. Coach Sherman knew his stuff and kept his sense of humor. Even to the very end of his regime. I liked him. He kept hollering a lot, but never viciously. He was more of a growler than a snarler. He wanted his fair advantage. He needed more than that. I never blamed a coach for looking for that extra edge.

One afternoon in Yankee Stadium the fans were quite demonstrative. That means they were yelling. Fortunately not at me, but at Coach Sherman. They wanted his ass—out of there. It was not his day. Nor the Giants' day. They were behind and nothing was breaking right. On fumbles the ball bounced away from the Giants' players. Right into the Cleveland team's hands. Flags were dropped, but most of the time against the Giants. Y. A. Tittle even got hurt that day.

The Giants were on a drive. First time that afternoon. Coach Allie Sherman yelled toward his team's huddle as they took a time-out. I thought the coach wanted to speak to me. I walked over and asked, "Do you want me, Coach?"

Allie Sherman took a long look at me. "You don't help me. You never did. Tell Tittle I want him. He can at least help me."

Coach Sherman sent in plays from the sideline. He used two guards as messengers. He was a good coach and his plays worked. Tittle drove the Giants down to the Cleveland two-yard line. Tittle was standing next to me as I gave the ready-to-play signal. No player was bringing in the play. Tittle kept staring at the sideline, trying to get Sherman's attention. Finally, Tittle turned to me and said, "Damn it. When we get close to the goal line, he forgets me."

I remember a backfield man, Joe Morrison, I think, who said, "Hell, he got you this far, Y. A. Now you're on your own."

Coach Sherman did send in a play. It worked too. For a touchdown. He knew his football and had a good sense of humor.

*   *   *

When I mention the Giants' coaches, I can't help but think of Father Dudley. He is not listed as a coach, but he follows the game closely as he stands on the sidelines. He has been with the Giants as far back as I can remember. A most unusual person, he travels with the Giants. If there is a fairer person around the League, then I haven't met him. He knows football; he is impartial and he never comments to the officials. Except for that one time.

There was a call against the Giants that hurt them. It was a tight ball game The lead had changed hands several times. It was tough all the way to the final whistle. As the six officials were running off the field and heading toward their dressing room, Father Dudley was waiting at the end of the field. He was shaking his head, apparently disgusted with the calls. I knew how he felt. As we ran by him, I waved at the six officials and said, "Father, safety in numbers."

He got a disgusted look and said, "You blew this one too, Norm. Safety is in Exodus."

The result of a game makes all the difference in the world to the coaches, and also to the others who follow the team. That was true of Father Dudley too. Especially after the Giants had defeated Pittsburgh in their must-win game. It assured the Giants a spot in the championship game a couple of weeks later. Y. A. Tittle had a great game. He had to, for Pittsburgh could have won that game. It was a tough game for either team to lose.

Dan Tehan was the head linesman that day. It was the end of a 33-year officiating career with few mistakes. He did another great job. We have to say that about one another. It's in our contracts. Not too many others say it, so we keep saying it. As Tehan and I were running off the field, Father Dudley was on the sideline, clapping his hands as we ran by.

"Great game, fellows, great game," he yelled at us. They are all great games when you win. But we believed Father Dudley. He hollered, "See you both in the championship game in Chicago in a couple of weeks."

No one knew who the officials would be for that game. The League office wouldn't let the officials know for another week. The reporters and television commentators wouldn't know until a couple of days prior to game time. I remember Tehan asking Father Dudley, "Father, are they making the assignments for that game out of your office?"

Both Tehan and I worked the championship game in Chicago two weeks later. Father Dudley had that knowing smile on his face when we saw him on the sideline the day of the game.

It isn't only the coaches who perform. Or coach. Everyone gets into the act. Even the doctors of the various football teams. They like to think they are coaching too. You would think that they have enough to do. But no. Some of them offer advice. Maybe I needed it over the years, but I sure got it in Detroit one day.

A Detroit player was hurt. Pretty bad too. Just one of those freak accidents that no one had any control over. That didn't stop the doctor. As he was treating the player, he kept up a vicious one-way conversation. He did all the talking.

"You're letting the game get away from you. You stink. You're no damn good." Some of the things he said are better left unsaid.

I looked down at the doctor. I had known him for years. Not once had I ever told him how to treat a player, offer advice on what was wrong or what I thought about an injury.

"Wait a second there, Doctor. Knock it off. Who the hell do you think you are? Finish your work and get off the field. You're just one of the team as far as I am concerned, so watch your language and what you say. I'll run your ass out of the park." I was hot.

The doctor was stunned. He should have been. He was way out of line. Perhaps he wanted to make amends when he said, "Heck, if a doctor makes a mistake, he's sorry. He can get sued for malpractice."

Who did he think he was fooling? "Listen," I told him, "if you make a mistake, you bury him. You got more bad calls in cemeteries than I have made in over twenty years. I have to live with my mistakes."

Gerry Hart was the umpire on our crew for the last number of years. A good official. Never backed up. As a result he was knocked on his ass a great number of times. I winced every time I saw him get hit and go down. But he bounced right up. He's big, tough, and goes around 260 pounds at 6 feet 3 inches.

The next time you watch a football game, keep an eye on the

umpire. He's the official who lines up three to five yards behind the defensive linemen. If you don't spot him right away, don't worry. You'll notice him when he picks himself up after being knocked down by a player. That's the umpire. He has to have eyes in the back of his head, and one in each ear. He's the original "Jack be nimble, Jack be quick." I wouldn't work that position for double my fee.

The New England Patriots were having a terrible time in Oakland a couple of seasons ago. Nothing went right for them. Their ends dropped passes with no one around them, their backs fumbled, tackles were missed and their blocks were high school blocks. They were caught holding a half-dozen times. Nothing clever or subtle in the way they grabbed Oakland players. They didn't even blame the officials. That's how tough things were for them.

Oakland's tight end Dave Casper slanted across the middle on a look-in pattern. He tried to use Gerry Hart, our umpire #62, as a post. Gerry Hart saw the tight end Casper coming right at him. Hart knew it was one of those "it's him or me" situations. Hart lowered his shoulder and knocked Casper on his rear.

I heard Chuck Fairbanks, coach of New England, yell at Hart, "Hey, Number Sixty-two, what do you weigh?"

Hart ignored him. He just watched the tight end try to get up.

"Hey, Number Sixty-two, what do you weigh? I want to know," Fairbanks yelled again.

Hart, who is big, turned and answered, "Two sixty-five." He is also built.

Fairbanks sighed. I heard it all the way to the center of the field. "Take off that damn striped shirt of yours and check out one of our uniforms. It's the first decent block I've seen today against Oakland. I'll call Rozelle and list the change."

It's nice to hear that from a coach who's losing. And going no place fast that day.

Coach Chuck Knox, then a big winner with the Los Angeles Rams and now with the Buffalo Bills, works hard and wants the officials to stay on top of the ball. That's fair enough. He just can't believe his team ever fouls. But then again, no coach believes his team ever fouls.

Gerry Hart and I walked out onto the field in Los Angeles one

Sunday afternoon. Hart was my umpire and a good one. Coach Knox met us on the sideline and told us, "You know, we have a football official work all our practices during the week. This official also reviews the rules and tells us what you men look for and how we can prevent fouls." Hart and I nodded.

It happened on the third play of the game. Hart called a holding penalty against the Rams. I heard Knox, clear out in the center of the field.

"Hart, how is it possible? We only had two fouls called against us the last game and also in the game before that. Two fouls, and you already have called one."

Hart yelled back as he picked up the flag, "Yeah, that's right. You still have one coming."

With some coaches it isn't what you know that keeps you out of trouble as a referee. It's what they think you know. Most coaches and players know that I edit the rule book, along with Art Mc-Nally. If it's a rule, I'm aware of it. Or should be. But that doesn't ensure the right call. That isn't found in any rule book.

A few years ago I had Detroit in New England. That was the game where George Ellis, the field judge, got run over by Lem Barney and had to be taken to the hospital immediately. We worked the game with one fewer official. We also were concerned about how George was and what was wrong with him. The president of the New England ball team, William Sullivan, showed class that day. In fact, he has shown class ever since he has been in the League. He made it a point to keep checking on Ellis while he was in the hospital. He also assured Ellis of care when he had to leave and fly back to Akron the next day where he lived. Mr. Sullivan couldn't do enough for the injured official. Different from what you might believe. A pro is a pro is a pro. And Sullivan is a pro.

This particular night New England was ahead by two points. Detroit had just completed a long pass to New England's 14-yard line. Only nine seconds showed on the stadium clock. And Detroit was out of time-outs. Suddenly a Detroit player staggered and fell down. Who knew whether he was faking? It didn't matter. As referee, I don't diagnose the injury. I just called time out for an injured player.

That stopped the clock. Both benches exploded. New England

was screaming, "Why did you stop the clock? The guy's faking it." Detroit was scurrying around, getting their field goal team set up. Lots of noise and activity out on the field. All directed at me.

The player jumped up and ran off the field. The Detroit center bent over the ball, ready to snap it. The place-kick holder was on one knee with his hands stretched out. Errol Mann was swinging his kicking foot, getting set to kick the ball. I was ready too. I told Hart, the umpire, "Keep your foot on the ball, Gerry. Don't let the snap get off until ten seconds have gone by."

I started the clock. Detroit went wild. The center tried to snap the ball, but Hart's foot was on the ball. And he has a big foot. At the end of nine seconds, the gun sounded. The game was over and no snap. I got the hell out of there. Fast.

I didn't get very far. When I got near the dressing room, Coach Joe Schmidt, of the Detroit Lions, was talking to Hart. They had played ball together for the Lions. Hart waved to me and beckoned, "Norm, tell Joe why you had me keep my foot on the ball."

I nodded and said, "Joe, if your team has an injury time-out in the last two minutes of a half, and you don't have time-outs left, we keep the clock running for ten seconds before you can snap the ball. That's only if the score is tied or if you are behind. That's to prevent phony injuries from stopping the clock. It's a rule. Since 1955."

Joe Schmidt was a helluva coach and guy. Never a problem and he understood the official's job. "I never heard of it, Norm. Are you sure it's in the book?"

"Dead sure, Joe. It's on page twenty-four. Right-hand side of the page."

Schmidt knew I worked closely with the rules and the rule book. He nodded and ran to his dressing room. It's a rule, all right. But I had the wrong page. Page 24, right-hand side of the book, sounded like a winning number at that time. I was close. It's on page 20 and on the left-hand side of the book. That's what I mean when I say it's what they think you know. It helps. Boy, how it helps!

I saw Frankie Albert's name in the papers the other day. Gosh, it's been a long time since I thought of him. It's been years since he last coached the San Francisco 49ers. He was another great player who turned coach. He did well. Even when things didn't go well, he never lost his sense of humor. And he had a good one. He took things in stride and didn't get too uptight. He didn't pop off at all.

He had a high draft choice one year who had been an All-American from Michigan. A great runner. On the first play of the rookie's first game, the rookie took the opening kickoff in the end zone. He started to come out onto the playing field about a foot or so. When he saw the other team charging at him, he realized that he should have downed the ball in his end zone for a touchback. This would have given the 49ers the ball on their 20-yard line with a first down. It was an automatic play for a veteran. Not for a rookie though.

Instead, the rookie went back into his end zone after he had gone out onto the field. He kneeled on the ground and downed the ball and then threw the ball to me in the end zone. That was a safety. It was a tough play for a rookie the first time he had played a pro game. He was quite disgusted with himself.

Coach Albert met him on the sideline. He placed his hand over the rookie's shoulders and calmly told him, "Don't worry, son. It isn't everyone who can score the first time he carries the ball in the National Football League."

We were working in old Kezar Stadium in San Francisco. There were always dozens of sea gulls flying around the stadium and over it. This particular day there were more sea gulls flying over the field than there were fans in the stands. And they had a good crowd that day.

Our field judge was Don Looney, a good one. Looney took things in stride. He was always in position, but never seemed to work too hard. When San Francisco took a time-out near their own goal line, Looney leaned against the goalpost and rested. Dan Tehan was standing next to Looney when Looney said, "Those sea gulls sure fly close to me. And they keep swooping over my head."

Tehan looked at the gulls diving near Looney and said, "Don, they're not sea gulls. They're buzzards. They think you're dead."

Looney ran a bit faster the second half.

You never really know how coaches feel about you as a referee. You really do, but you pretend a lot when you are a professional football referee. I remember one night in Salt Lake City. It was a pre-season game and the New York Giants were one of the teams. I think Baltimore was the other club. Frank Gifford was in his heyday as a player then. Two things happened that night which I remember quite vividly. I don't remember who won. I don't even remember what kind of a game it was or how it went.

Jim Lee Howell was the coach of the Giants then. Jim Lee liked to help the referee. That fair advantage looked good to him. One time the line play was rough. I threw my flag for offensive holding. I marched off 15 yards against the Giants. It had happened right in front of the Giants' bench. One of the assistant coaches yelled, "Let's use some common sense out there."

Howell looked at me and bellowed, "If he had any common sense, he wouldn't be out there."

The other incident involved Frank Gifford. The Colts had the ball on the Giants' eight-yard line. John Unitas didn't try for a field goal. Even though it was fourth down. Instead he went for the touchdown. He threw a short pass over the middle which hit the ground around the two-yard line and then rolled into the end zone. At that time the rule stated, "Any incomplete forward pass on fourth down in the opponents' end zone is a touchback." That meant that the ball would be then spotted on the 20-yard line and given over to the Giants. The rule has since been changed. It is no longer a touchback, but goes back to the previous spot. That's where the center snapped the ball.

When Unitas' thrown ball hit on the two-yard line of the Giants and rolled into the end zone, I put the ball back on the eight-yard line. I signaled first down for the Giants. I heard a roar from the Giants' sideline. I spotted Coach Howell yelling at Gifford. Howell was pointing and talking at the same time.

Gifford had his instructions and came running onto the field. He ran right to me. "Hey, Norm. It's a touchback. The ball was in the end zone. We want the ball on the twenty-yard line."

I shook my head. "No way, Frank. The ball has to land in the end zone."

Gifford didn't give up. He never did. I mean as a runner or a receiver. "The ball went into the end zone. It rolled in."

"Rollies don't count, Frank. It has to hit the ground first in the end zone. Ball's on the eight-yard line," I shouted. I wanted Howell on the sideline to hear me.

Whether Howell did or didn't hear me didn't matter. The ball went on the eight-yard line. Every time I see Gifford now, I think of rollies. Rollies! Where did that come from in my childhood?

Talk about elephants never forgetting. I'll stack any coach in the NFL against any elephant. Especially if they think a call went against them.

I was sitting in the press box at Denver's Mile High Stadium, observing the officials for the League office. Dick Nolan, former head coach of the San Francisco 49ers, was sitting next to me. He was scouting for the Oakland Raiders. He was getting a line on Denver. This was before he went to coach the New Orleans Saints.

Sometime in the second quarter, Steve Ramsey, the Denver quarterback, was about to be trapped for a heavy loss. Suddenly the ball was flipped and landed about 10 yards past the scrimmage line with no players of either team anywhere near the spot where the ball landed. Nolan swung around toward me. "Norm, wasn't that intentional grounding?"

I kept my eyes on the field. I didn't see any flag. "I guess not, Dick. I don't see a flag down on the field. If it was grounding, the flag would be down."

Nolan kept looking at me. "Norm, I remember a similar situation in San Francisco about five years ago. Exactly the same play. And you called intentionally grounding on Brodie. How come?"

Five years ago! In San Francisco! Hell, I don't even remember where I was last week. I don't even remember who's playing the day I am working the game. If I remembered all the calls I made, I would go out of my mind. I wouldn't be able to find my way to next week's game. And I have my schedule right in front of me.

I can remember sitting in Hopkins Airport, Cleveland, late one Sunday afternoon after a tough ball game. Jack Faulkner, a good friend since he came into the League as an assistant coach in 1955, came walking in with several other Ram assistant coaches. I was sipping a short one. The Ram coaches had been quite verbal that afternoon. Nothing personal, but bitch-bitch-bitch all game long. Just a typical Sunday afternoon for a referee in the NFL.

Faulkner has been a friend for well over 20 years. Probably

knows as much football as anyone in the League. He has been a head coach, an assistant coach and a special coach and coordinator. He has done it all. And good too. Probably screamed as loud as anyone else. But a real nice fellow. Likable, enjoyable, good company and completely honest. But that day wasn't one for conversation. With anyone. At least not for me. I had had it. Up to here.

Faulkner saw me at the table, waved and came over to talk. He started right in. I didn't expect a "Nice game, Norm," but the game was over. The Rams had won, and I had had no calls that had any bearing on the ball game. In fact, I figured I had had a good day. But the coaches had been vocal. Both sides. They must have thought that the louder they screamed, the more breaks would go their way. Hell, it never works that way. Sometimes the coaches never come up for air, and that's when we get a bit peeved. Isn't peeved a nice word? Pissed off is more like it.

Anyway, Faulkner walked up to the table where Fette, Connell, Rohrig and I were sitting. There was an empty chair and he sat down. "Mind if I sit down? And talk?"

I looked at Faulkner. "Jack, you talked all afternoon. You probably haven't anything new to say. Hell, we may have to work with you, but we don't have to drink with you."

I was kidding in a half-ass way. Faulkner looked surprised. He started to get up. "Sit down, Jack. I'm kidding. You're one of the good guys. You know what it's all about. Be our guest."

A referee has to be careful whom he sits with, eats with or spends time with. Football coaches are suspicious people. If one of them sees you with another coach, he immediately thinks you're being briefed or debriefed. And quite often you are. That is especially true on the ball field, prior to a game, or at half time. Whenever a coach corners a referee and starts talking and gesturing, the other coach always manages to come up. If he doesn't, and the referee doesn't go to him for a few minutes of reciprocal conversation, then he thinks he's been had. As a rule, I never talked to either coach before the game unless I had them both together.

Emil "Dutch" Heintz once told me of an incident that happened to him in Wrigley Field. It helps illustrate what I have just been trying to say. It goes back a number of years, even before I got into the League as a referee. That's a lot of years ago. But it shows how coaches work. Work the officials, I mean. Sometimes it backfires, but if it's worth a laugh, it's worth remembering.

Dutch Heintz was a damn good referee. Excellent. One of the very best that ever put on a uniform with stripes. Strong-willed, hard-nosed, never-bending and a stickler for principles. A great referee. He had had many a run-in with George Halas over the years. Nothing vicious. Each respected the other, but they would go head to head many times. Heintz once told me of an afternoon that had its moments in Wrigley Field.

Charlie Berry was his head linesman. Berry was also one of baseball's better umpires during the summer months. He had been a big league catcher for years before he went into umpiring full time. He was a good one too. He had smarts as an official. Never ruffled, always on the ball and always a word to say to anybody. And said it. Kept himself and others loose. We also worked together for a number of years. I liked Berry.

This particular afternoon Halas kept blasting Berry. Unmercifully. Kept referring to Berry as "Hey, you baseball ump." It didn't bother Charlie though. He knew all the tricks in Halas' bag. Berry laughingly gave back as much as he took. It was almost a standoff. After a sideline call by Berry against the Bears, Halas went sky-high. It was an act. But it annoyed Heintz, who didn't like that kind of an act. Dutch knew that the officials would catch hell after that. It was a game with Halas, and a bigger one with Berry. He enjoyed the byplay and didn't pay any attention to it. Charlie figured it was all a part of an afternoon's work. He had worked thousands of big league baseball games and hundreds of pro football games. No strain, no pain for Berry.

Heintz was a different breed of official. He watched Halas and Berry's performance. He wanted to bring it to a close, so he walked over to the sideline to break it up and to get the game going again. Berry didn't throw his penalty flag, for he enjoyed the discussion. Heintz didn't want it to develop into anything more serious, so he got closer to Halas than he should have done. When he got to Halas, Halas reached over and put his arm around Heintz's shoulders in a friendly gesture.

Heintz shook Halas' arm off him and threw his penalty flag. "That will cost you fifteen yards."

Heintz walked off the 15 yards. Halas was speechless. Almost. Before long, he recovered and started to howl. "Emil, what's the flag for? Nothing happened. What the hell are you doing. I was showing you that I had no hard feelings against you."

Dutch Heintz looked through Halas. "George, no way are you going to blast Berry, yell at him, and then come over to me in front of all these hometown fans, put your arm around me and hint that I'm your friend and that Berry knows nothing. That's unsportsmanlike conduct. Fifteen yards."

This time Halas was speechless. Really. No way will you find that penalty in the rule book.

That's why Heintz was a great one. He adjusted himself and the rules to situations. That's what they pay for. They got their money's worth with Dutch Heintz. So did I, for I broke in on his crew. What a blessing. Especially for a rookie official.

When I joined Heintz's crew he told me, "Norm, just remember two things. Just two. That's all. First, don't ever blow your whistle unless you see the ball. That cuts out those inadvertent whistles you read about. Second thing to remember is, Is it right or wrong? Remember those two things and you'll stay around for a long time."

It's a funny thing how certain situations that happened with coaches stick with a referee. Notice that I didn't say "hang with the referee." I can still remember a certain assistant coach in Pittsburgh years ago. Two years or so after I had been hired as an official in the NFL, I was moved to the referee position. It was at that time that my first English textbook had been published. The galley proofs were still in my mind as I blew the whistle for the opening kickoff in Pittsburgh. Nice day, if I remember correctly. They were all nice days, especially before kickoff time.

One of the assistant coaches had been needling me from the sideline. One of the papers had written up a short item that I had had a book published. So the coach was letting me have it. "Say something in English, Ref. You wrote the book. You're the expert on grammar and spelling. You can't see, but you can write." The coach ended his little monologue with "You blind sonavabitch."

I had enjoyed all the word byplay. But not his last "You blind sonavabitch." Hell, he said that I was the expert on spelling and grammar. I had heard him. I looked over at the coach and walked over to the bench. (Incidentally, that assistant coach became a head coach for two different clubs later on.)

"Coach, tell me something," I asked, "is sonavabitch a hyphenated word? Is it one word or three words? I can't remember, for sure."

The coach looked me up and down. And then sideways. One of those "You stupid shit" looks they throw around. "What the shit difference does it make? One or three words? How the hell do I know? I didn't write the book. You did, you blind sonavabitch."

I nodded. "That's right. I wrote the book. It's going to cost you five yards a word. The way you pronounced son-of-bitch, it's three words. That's fifteen yards—against you."

I walked off the 15 yards. When the press questioned my call after the game, and wondered what I had called unsportsmanlike conduct for, I just said, "The coach used three words instead of one. He could have saved ten yards if he had read my book."

Roughing the Passer

No matter how many times I fly across the country, the snow-capped mountains in Utah take my breath away. Simply unbelievable. So high, so cold, so remote. A forest ranger in such a remote area must have a tough job. Then I think about my job as a football referee. I don't know which job is tougher. I am certain that nobody, I mean nobody, is looking over the shoulder of a forest ranger and second-guessing him. I'm positive that 60,000,000 television viewers don't watch him work. He has serenity, peace and loneliness—three things I don't have after the opening kickoff of the first game. Anyway, when I see those spectacular mountains and remote wilderness, I realize that my calls on the professional football field are not that important or earth-shattering. There must be 400,000,000 Chinese who don't even know that I work football, or who won the big game last Sunday afternoon.

On my flight to Super Bowl X, I was thinking of the seclusion of those mountains in contrast to the chaos of some Sunday afternoons when the close calls bring the fans to their feet and the coaches two feet off the ground.

No calls are easy. When that flag goes down, some team is going to pay for its mistake. Yardage comes tough in this league. Any yardage you hand over to the other team is bitterly contested by the player who made the foul. To say nothing of the way the coach reacts. "Bitterly contested" means the player and coach bitch like hell. The day that fouls become automatic to a referee, he'd better think of calling it a day. He won't have to, for someone will think of it for him. The football takes funny bounces. It's those bounces, besides the calls, that create problems. And laughs. A referee better laugh, even to himself, when the laugh is there.

Look at the referee the next time you watch a pro football game. He's the guy in the striped shirt behind the quarterback. He baby-sits the quarterback. At least that's what some defensive players say. And they are right. The quarterback is a valuable commodity. He is in a vulnerable position as he sets up to throw the ball. His primary objective is to spot an open receiver. He concentrates on completing the forward pass and is often off-balance when he is throwing the ball. He never looks at the onrushing defensive tackles and ends, to say nothing about the blitzing linebackers. The defensive team's job is to keep the quarterback honest and gun-shy. They tell him, "You're going to get creamed." My job is to see that the quarterback stays in one piece. And doesn't get creamed.

A difficult call for the referee is when the quarterback sets up to throw the ball. Suppose a defensive tackle breaks through, hits the quarterback from the blind side, and the ball pops out of the quarterback's hand. Is it a fumble or an incomplete pass? Oh, boy, is there a difference!

It sounds simple, but you can't win. No matter what you rule, 50 percent of the coaches and players think you blew the call. The coaches and players on the other side of the field think it was a great call.

Watch the referee set up on a forward pass play. He stands on the quarterback's right side. That gives him a good look at the quarterback's arm. Of course, if it's a left-handed quarterback, like Ken Stabler or Jim Zorn, a referee sets up on the man's left side. An experienced referee watches the quarterback's hand all the way. If his hand was coming forward in a throwing motion when he was hit and the ball falls to the ground, then it is an incomplete pass. If the ball was still in the quarterback's hand when he was tackled and the ball then falls out of his hand and hits the ground, it is a fumble. It is a bang-bang look and call. No committee meetings, no film playbacks (there is later after the game, but by then it is too late) and no "Let me see it one more time, please." It's bang-bang. Fumble or incomplete pass?

The smart quarterbacks, and they are all smart or they wouldn't be in this league, learn early in their careers that anytime they are hit while trying to throw a pass, bring the hand down as if following through on a forward pass motion. When that play happens (and it does several times a ball game), then watch the referee. He will be looking at the quarterback's throwing hand and nothing else at that time to determine whether or not it is a legitimate attempt to pass. He also has to watch to see if the quarterback is hit again by some other player. That becomes roughing the passer.

It was a typical Green Bay Packers and Baltimore Colts game, being played in Baltimore in Memorial Stadium, the largest outdoor insane asylum in the country. The noise level blows your mind. The fans there let you know when they are unhappy with your call. All 60,000 of them. "Let you know" is a mild way of saying that 60,000 Colts fans are yelling, "Kill that sonavabitch."

There is no easy Packers-Colts game. Never has been. Not for me anyway. And I have worked almost two dozen of them. This game was no exception. I had two tough "Is it a fumble or an incomplete pass?" calls. Both against the Colts, the home team. It seems to work that way.

John Unitas, the Colts' quarterback then, was the best. That's what I think. And I've worked them all for 22 years. A smart quarterback is always thinking. That's what I liked about John Unitas. He was thinking all the time. He was a gentleman, but that didn't stop him from trying to outsmart the referee.

Unitas was hit from the blind side as he was setting up to throw a pass. If his hand was coming down and the ball dropped out of his hand, then it was an incomplete pass. If the ball was knocked out of his hand before his hand was coming down, then it was a fumble. I had to give it a good look and to be in position. I did and I was. Just as Unitas was hit from the side, the ball dropped out of his hand. Just as soon as the ball dropped from his hand, Unitas brought his right hand forward. It was a bang-bang play and move.

I ruled it a fumble and let the play develop. The Packers recovered. Unitas rushed me and said, "My hand was coming down. It is an incomplete pass. No way a fumble if my hand was coming down."

I agreed with Unitas. "That's right, John, your hand was coming down. But the ball has to be in it."

Unitas smiled and walked away. He was thinking all the time. The fans let me have it. They didn't see Unitas smile. And they weren't thinking.

It always happens. If one call goes against the home team, something will happen soon after that will also go against the home team. They say it all evens out, but not for the referee. On the very next series of downs after the fumble recovery by the Packers (that I ruled fumble), Green Bay had the ball. On the second down, Bart Starr (the second best quarterback that I have ever seen and then the Packers' quarterback) dropped back to pass and was hit from the blind side just as his arm was coming down. The ball went forward right in front of him. I blew my whistle and immediately signaled an incomplete pass.

The Colts' defensive tackle, #76, picked up the ball and started to run for a touchdown. I blew my whistle again and then again. I yelled, "Incomplete pass, incomplete." I didn't want him to go all the way for a score and have to bring the ball back. I would never get out of there that day.

Number 76 hesitated and yelled back, "Fumble, fumble!" He started to run again.

I blew my whistle harder and shouted, "Fumble, my ass. It's an incomplete pass. Give me that ball."

Number 76 stopped and got a hurt and disappointed look on his face. He ran up to me and said, "Mr. Referee, you shouldn't talk that way. It's not nice."

I was stunned. Here was this 6-foot 7-inch tackle about 270 pounds upset about my saying "ass." I felt foolish and ashamed. "Say, I'm sorry. I should never have used that word. Forgive me. I lost my head."

He agreed, dropped the ball right on my foot and said, "That's better, you sonavabitch."

A fumbled ball creates havoc for everyone, and particularly for the referee. Whenever there was a fumble in a tight ball game, all hell broke loose. It never seemed to be a clear-cut fumble recovery, one in which a player would recover the ball out in the open. There was generally a pileup, with the ball at the bottom of the pile, where it had been changing hands several times before the players could be untangled. The player finally with the ball was given possession. And that's when the boo-birds started their song.

Howard Cosell brought a moment of great sadness to me one Monday night when I was sitting at home watching the game.

I had worked the day before in Green Bay. Oakland had been in there banging heads with the Packers. In the second quarter MacArthur Lane of the Packers had taken a pitchout from his quarterback Scott Hunter. Lane received the ball around the 10-yard line and ran for the goal line. I kept my eyes on Scott Hunter as some extra-curricular activity was developing. When I looked to my right, MacArthur Lane was past the scrimmage line, which had been around the five-yard line. Lane couldn't quite find the handle to the ball. It finally fell out of his hands two yards past the scrimmage line. That meant that Lane had had the ball for seven yards. The ball rolled into the end zone. Jack Tatum, of Oakland, picked up the loose ball four yards deep in his own end zone and ran 104 yards for an Oakland touchdown. That was a new NFL record. It was the longest yardage ever recorded returning a fumble. It knocked right out of the record book George Halas' run of a fumbled ball of 98 yards set back in 1923. That was when the Chicago Bears played the Oorang Indians in Marion, Ohio. That's right. The Oorang Indians. That should give you some idea of how long Halas' record has been in the record book.

At half time David "Red" Hanner, the Packers' assistant coach, knocked on our dressing room door. He yelled, "Norm, can I speak with you?"

It was a small room, so when the door was opened, we visited. "Norm, I want to talk to you about that backward pass that Tatum recovered and ran for a touchdown. Who made that call? Why wasn't it blown dead when Tatum picked up the ball?"

"No backward pass, Red. It was a fumbled ball. The head linesman was right on the play. Followed it all the way."

The head linesman spoke up. "It was a fumble. MacArthur had had possession of the ball before he dropped it. He ran about five yards with the ball."

That ended the conversation. For that time.

On Monday night following our game on Sunday, Howard Cosell ran that play. Five times. Over and over again. It was the same ending every single time. MacArthur Lane had taken a backward pass and started to run. When he dropped the ball, he already had run past the scrimmage line. The head linesman had a good look at the play, believed that Lane had had control of the ball, and had dropped the ball after he had run five yards. The films showed that Lane never really had complete possession. It was a bang-bang call and made with no hesitation. The official couldn't see the ball moving in Lane's hands, as Lane's body covered the action. It looked like a routine, completed backward pass and then a fumble.

Just a quick word about a fumble and a backward pass. A fumble recovered by any player of either team may be advanced. A backward pass recovered by a defensive player may only be recovered and not advanced. The play is dead where the ball is recovered. That would have given Oakland a touchback, not a touchdown. And George Halas would still be in the record book.

It was like something out of a movie. Oakland was in San Diego, with the Chargers leading by a score of 20–14. It was second down for Oakland with the ball on San Diego's 14-yard line. Oakland needed a touchdown and the extra point to win. And there was only time left for one last play.

Everybody in the country knew the last play would be a forward pass. It had to be. Ken Stabler, quarterback of Oakland then, took the center snap, dropped back and looked for any open receiver to catch the do-or-die touchdown pass. Stabler was tackled from his blind side, and the ball popped out of his hand and flew forward six yards. Did he flip the ball underhand, or was it knocked loose and become a fumble?

The ball hit the ground on the eight-yard line. Bradshaw, one of Oakland's ends, tried to pick up the ball but couldn't get the handle to it. The ball went forward after he tried to pick it up. Dave Casper, Oakland's tight end then, accidentally kicked the loose ball on the eight-yard line right into San Diego's end zone. An Oakland player fell on the ball there.

Touchdown! Or was it? Was it a fumble or an incomplete pass? The referee was in the right spot—standing on Stabler's left side because Stabler was a left-handed passer. The referee had the best view in the country, and saw the entire action. Time had run out on the play. However, as the play had started with time remaining, the line judge didn't shoot his gun until the entire play had finished. The entire controversial play occurred after time had run out.

The referee ruled fumble. His decision was the only one that counted. He was there, he saw it and ruled on it immediately. All hell broke loose on the field after his ruling. Coach Tommy Prothro, his assistants and all the San Diego players were yakking at the referee. Right out on the field. I was sitting in the press box, observing the game for the League. I knew exactly what was being said out on the field. I had gone through all that conversation. Many, many times.

Finally, the referee cleared the field. The fans in the stands kept screaming. Score was now 20–20. Even though time had expired in the ball game, the rules state "If a touchdown is made on the last play of a period, the try-for-point shall be allowed."

Imagine the tension on that extra-point try. I could well appreciate how the referee felt. Though there was no hesitation in his decision, no doubt in his mind, he had to be thinking. He saw a fumble, and that was the call. Oakland kicked the extra point and won the game 21–20. Picture the referee and his crew running for the dressing room. In San Diego. All of them made it. Just barely.

Reporters in the press box rushed over to Sid Gillman, who was scouting for the Houston Oilers. Coach Gillman had been one of the truly outstanding coaches in professional football since 1955, when he started with the Los Angeles Rams. And took them to a championship. His teams won 115 games. Gillman was sitting in the row above me in the press box. I heard him tell the reporters, "Don't ask me. Ask Norm. He's right there. He's seen hundreds of those calls. Had to rule on them."

Coach Gillman was right. I had seen hundreds of them. And all of them were tough calls. Not to me, or to any other referee, at the time it happened. We called what we saw. The writers came over to me. I closed my notebook, for I had already made my notations on my report for the League. Finally, one of the writers said, "You saw it, Norm. How about it? Fumble or incomplete pass?"

"I report to the League office. Please check with them."

I made my way down to the officials' dressing room. By the time I·got there, the pool reporter (the one who represents all the writers) had just finished getting the answers from the referee. It was still a fumble call.

When I entered the dressing room (after showing lots of NFL identification to the policeman at the door), no one was talking. Fifty-nine minutes and 59 seconds of the game were played without a problem. Then bang! On the last play in the last second everything turned upside down. Not that the call was wrong. Just that it was so close. When I walked in, the officials looked over at me.

I said, "Nice game, fellows."

"Did you see the play on instant replay upstairs? How did it look to you, Norm?"

"I saw it. Several times. But the replay didn't show anything. It was a gutsy call—and a good one." I stopped for a second, and then turned to the referee and said, "If people didn't know you were working in the League before today, they'll know you tomorrow."

The referee knew I wasn't doubting or questioning his call. No official second-guesses another official. The person who had been in the best position to make that call was the referee on the play —and he was in great position and looking in. All I was saying was that good or bad, it was so close that it would be kicked around by everyone. And it was.

Most people who watched the game, either in the stadium or around the country on television, didn't realize at the time that we had a fourth-down fumble rule in the book. The rule stated, "Any player who fumbles on fourth-down within the opponents' 10-yard line is the only player of the fumbling team who can recover that fumbled ball." It was a good rule, for it prevented a runner who had been stopped short of the goal line on fourth down to fumble the ball deliberately or accidentally and hope that his teammate would recover the ball in the end zone.

That rule didn't help the officials on Stabler's play. It had been only second down and outside of the 10-yard line. However, the following year the Competition Committee of the NFL suggested a change in the fumble rule. The Competition Committee is composed of Tex Schramm of Dallas, Paul Brown of Cincinnati, Eddie LeBaron of Atlanta and Don Shula of Miami. All are solid rules people and have been around the League for a long, long time. The League owners approved the fumble rule change.

Now the fumble rule states, "If a fourth-down fumble occurs during a play from scrimmage, the fumbling player is the only player of his team who may recover and advance the ball." They added a supplemental note to the rule which states, "Any fumble that occurs during a down after the two-minute warning may not be advanced by any member of the fumbling team except the player who fumbled the ball."

With the new rule there wouldn't have been any close call on Stabler's play. It wouldn't have mattered if it was a fumble or an incomplete pass as it had occurred in the last two minutes. If that play happens today, no problem. The game would be over when the ball was recovered. San Diego would have won 20–14.

Coach Tommy Prothro of the Chargers resigned two weeks after that play. Don Coryell took over as head coach. He finished the season. The next July I went to the San Diego Chargers' training camp to give them the annual rules talk. My talk was scheduled right after lunch. I was having some dessert with the coaches before my talk, when Jerry Smith, the defensive line coach of the Chargers, asked, "What are you going to talk about today, Norm?"

"The new fumble rule. We put in a new one in this year's rule book."

"Hell, Norm. That call last year changed our season."

Don Coryell, the new head coach, said, "That was a tough call for us to take."

Before he could say another word, I interrupted. "Coach, if that call hadn't happened, you wouldn't be head coach now."

Coryell grinned and said, "Nobody say another word."

Walter Payton, great back of the Chicago Bears, is a certain Hall of Famer. He can't miss. A great guy. He also has a keen sense of humor that makes working in the NFL so different. Last season a close call by Ed Marion on a fumble by Payton on Atlanta's two-yard line created the longest and loudest rhubarb of the year.

The Chicago Bears were driving for a score. Payton took the ball and drove into the scrimmage line. He was tackled and fell to the ground. That's when all hell popped. Marion, one of the best head linesman in football, saw Payton lose the ball before his shoulder or knee touched the ground. The ball was up for grabs. The Falcons fell on it. Payton couldn't believe the call. He felt he dropped the ball after his knee had touched the ground. The *before* or *after* is what created the controversy. If the ball had become loose before Payton hit the ground, it was a fumble. And a great call. It was another of those bang-bang calls that have to be made as it happens. If Payton had hit the ground and then lost the ball, it would not have been a fumble. Atlanta would have recovered a dead ball, because the play would have ended when Payton was legally down. Chicago would have kept the ball with another chance to score.

Payton couldn't and wouldn't believe the call. He ran up to Marion and tried to get his attention. He made the mistake of shoving Marion by laying a hand on him in a visible manner which might have been misinterpreted by the fans. That is an automatic disqualification penalty. Marion ran Payton out of the game. That's when the roof came down.

Reporters, television commentators and everyone who watched the game got into the act. I remember being in New Orleans for the Monday night game following the play on Sunday. I was in the press box and saw ABC run the play several times during half time, but nothing was conclusive.

The League office studied the CBS film coverage of Payton's play, along with additional footage from the NFL films. The League issued a statement on Thursday that it was not a fumble, but Payton should not have jostled Marion. Instant replay would not have helped that Sunday afternoon, the day of the game. Nothing showed up conclusively, except for Payton's shoving Marion. When a reporter called Marion after the League announcement and asked, "What do you say now about your fumble call?" Marion didn't hesitate. "I had to make my call Sunday afternoon the way I saw it. I couldn't wait to make it on Thursday morning."

Walter Payton and Ed Marion always joked and kidded one another. Just before the Chicago-Atlanta game that day, Marion walked up to Payton and told him, "No untying shoelaces today, Walter."

Payton laughed. He told Marion, "You got to have a little fun."

What brought on that conversation of shoelaces being untied was a little byplay that happened a year or so ago during a game between Chicago and Minnesota. The first time Payton carried the ball he was tackled near Marion's position. There was the usual pileup and untangling of bodies to get the ball. As Marion reached in to get the ball, he saw a hand reach out from the bottom of the pile and untie his shoelaces.

Marion followed the moving hand and saw it belonged to Payton. "What the hell are you doing, Walter?"

"I untied your shoelaces," Payton answered as he ran back to the huddle.

Five minutes later Marion was reaching for the ball again. Payton had carried it. Ed saw Payton's hand start toward his laces again. "Knock that stuff off, Walter. I'll stick you fifteen yards."

Both of them laughed. Payton again ran back to his huddle. When Payton did the untying-the-shoelaces routine again for the third time, Marion told him, "I told you I would stick you fifteen." But he didn't throw his flag. It was a joke between the two of them.

Payton patted Marion on his stomach and once again ran back to the Bears' huddle. Soon afterward Payton took a hand-off and ran out of bounds on Marion's sideline. Marion marked the out-of-bounds spot with his foot. Payton stood about one and a half yards ahead of Marion's mark. Payton looked at Marion, pointed to where he was standing and said, "Here's the right spot."

Marion didn't even look at Payton. "No, it's back here, Walter."

Payton repeated where he thought the spot was. And Marion kept pointing to his spot. Then Payton ran up to Marion and patted him on the stomach. "You're slowing up, Ed. You should lose some weight."

Marion smiled and yelled back, "The next time it will be twenty-five yards, not fifteen."

Both the referee and the quarterback are vital to the operation of the ball game. The quarterback is the engineer who moves the team to where it should go—the other team's goal line. The referee is the safety check (or maintenance man) who sees that things move smoothly, don't break down, and everyone plays by the rules.

Intentional grounding of the football is always a controversial call. No one on the offensive team is happy with the call. Even when it is obvious, the quarterback screams and rants and pouts. He "pouts" by pointing his finger at the referee in such a way that he seems to be signifying "You stupid bastard. You haven't the brains of a jackass."

Intentional grounding is a forward pass from behind the line that is intentionally thrown to the ground in order to escape loss of yardage. It's a judgment call. Purely judgment on the part of the referee. Anytime a referee has to read intent into a player's action, there's a problem.

The veteran quarterbacks are clever about unloading the ball. Years ago they tried to get rid of the ball by throwing it near a defensive man—far enough away so he couldn't intercept the ball. Seldom was intentional grounding called. Nowadays we don't have those escape guidelines. If a referee thinks the quarterback intended to save yardage by flipping the ball away—bang! there goes the penalty flag. That's when it becomes interesting.

The Dallas Cowboys and the Philadelphia Eagles were really having at it. Dallas was mad, and Philadelphia felt as if the world and the officials were against them, and I knew that my luck had run out. Worse yet, I was wearing a NBC mike as they were taping me for a national TV segment for "Grandstand," their half-time show. They had to be delighted with what was said on the field. I was lucky NBC took out part of the following incident when they played it at half time.

Roman Gabriel, quarterback of the Eagles and a friend for many years, had been around for a long time. He was smart. I knew him and his habits quite well. He was a past master at unloading the ball. On second down and long yardage, Gabriel dropped back to pass. He was trapped. As he was being tackled, he flipped the ball downfield. His head was close to the ground and facing away from the direction of the pass. He was lucky to unload the ball.

I glanced downfield, saw no player near the spot where the ball was going to land, and threw my penalty flag for intentional grounding of the ball. Just as I threw my flag, Harold Carmichael, the tall end for the Eagles, dived for the ball and didn't miss by much. Without thinking and forgetting that I was on live for NBC, I said, "Where the shit did he come from?"

I didn't get an answer. Gabriel was all over me, shouting, screaming, swearing, and complaining about the intentional grounding foul I had just called against him. "Norm, you're wrong again."

The "again" pissed me off. I yelled back, "Roman, your head was up your ass when you threw that ball. Get away from me." His teammates had to hold him back. And all this action was being taped for the half-time TV show.

It always happens. On the very next play, the very next play, Randy White, the strong linebacker for Dallas, blitzed and hit Gabriel right in the chops. Smack in the face. My flag hit the ground just as White's forearm went across Gabriel's helmet. "Keep away from his head. That's roughing the passer," I yelled.

They can't rough the passer. That would give the Eagles a first down and 15 yards assessed against Dallas. Lee Roy Jordan, the captain of Dallas, rushed in and shouted, "Norm, are you making up for that last call you made against the Eagles with this one?"

I looked at Jordan and without realizing that I was being taped and was on live answered, "Lee Roy, I never even up my calls on the next play. I usually wait at least two or three plays before I even it up."

Can you imagine that being taped? It did not go out live to the country, but it did go to the League office.

That wasn't the only thing that went back to the League office. Dallas kicked a field goal in the last few seconds to beat Philadelphia. The gun had sounded as the ball was in the air. It looked like a movie script. The Eagle fans were furious. Furious is a mild word for how they felt. A game was just taken away from them. Not so much by a better team, but by those shittin' officials. At least that was the feeling of the fans as we ran off the field. Most of the fans anyway. I think Gerry Hart, the umpire, had a couple of his cousins at the game who used his tickets. Come to think of it, we never did see his cousins after the game.

The next morning I called Art McNally, the Supervisor of Officials, to give my report on the previous day's game. Every Monday morning, all referees call McNally to brief him on any problem calls that might have been made. This is to alert him of possible phone calls from coaches and reporters. I told McNally, "Routine game, Art. No problems. Easy game." That's the way I had seen it.

Some fellows never get the word. That's what I heard in the Marine Corps. And it's probably true for referees. McNally stopped me with "I hate to tell you this, Norm. But your crew knocked the war off the front pages in Philadelphia. There are pictures of some of the crew members climbing into the stands and swinging at the fans. I hate to think of what it would have been like if you had had a problem."

Art sent the pictures. Hart was climbing the wall to get at

someone who had spilled beer all over his head. Fette was throwing a can back at a fan who had hit him with it. Come to think of it, none of us took a good picture.

Funny how some plays stick in a referee's mind. I can still remember Y. A. Tittle running for his life most of an afternoon against the Chicago Bears. Bill George and Joe Fortunato were all over Tittle. If I didn't know that they were defensive linebackers for the Bears, I would have thought that they were running backs for the Giants. They were in the Giants' backfield all afternoon.

Once Tittle was trapped about 20 yards back of his scrimmage line. He was almost tackled by Bill George, who kept chasing Tittle all over the field. Tittle started to run toward the sideline. George was breathing down Tittle's neck. I was trailing both of them. Not too far away though. Instead of running out of bounds 20 yards behind the line of scrimmage, Tittle gambled on my not making a call. He threw the ball downfield about 50 yards. It landed just inside the sideline. No one was nearer than 30 yards to it. Tittle lost his gamble. I threw my flag for intentional grounding. That cost the Giants 15 yards and a down.

Tittle charged me. "Norm, I was throwing to Shofner. It was a busted play. He just cut the wrong way."

"I'll say he did, Y. A. He was forty yards from the ball. If you don't throw any better than that, you'll be gone before the season ends."

Y. A. Tittle was voted the most valuable player in the League that year. That's why nobody ever asks me to scout football players, especially quarterbacks.

Tittle's passes in the championship game against the Bears weren't the best he ever threw. The Bears intercepted five of them, and turned two of them into touchdowns and won the game 14–10. That was just one game. Usually, Y. A. could thread a needle. I mean with his forward passes. He took his time though. Too much time for a referee to have a good day. Tittle didn't throw the ball until the last split second, just as the defensive man crashed into him. There was no way the defensive man could avoid him. Players like George, Karras, Nitschke, Bednarik and Schmidt were always banging into Tittle. Every time Tittle went back to pass, a defensive player would be all over him. He would

George Halas has a special spot in my memories.
VERNON J. BIEVER PHOTO, COURTESY NFL PROPERTIES

*Unless you have been chewed out by
Coach Vince Lombardi, you haven't
really been chewed out.*
NATE FINE PHOTO

They don't come much better than John Madden.
PHOTO BY MALCOLM W. EMMONS

Coach Don Shula has mellowed over the years.
PHOTO BY JOHN RIMKUS, MIAMI NEWS

*You always knew where you stood
with Coach Van Brocklin.*
PHOTO BY MALCOLM W. EMMONS

*Paul Brown never swore . . . and I
gave him many opportunities . . .*
PHOTO BY MALCOLM W. EMMONS

The close call that created the longest and loudest rhubarb of the year 1980—the Walter Payton fumble controversy. WIDE WORLD PHOTOS

How could anyone think Y. A. Tittle was not being fouled repeatedly?
PHOTO BY MORRIS BERMAN, PITTSBURGH POST-GAZETTE

Eddie LeBaron was a magician with the ball. Here he is with Coach Tom Landry on December 2, 1962, Cowboys 45–Browns 21.
NFL PROPERTIES PHOTO

I wonder what I was saying to Otto Graham right after One-Punch Hensley decked a fan. UPI PHOTO

I didn't like to irritate Dick Butkus. NFL PROPERTIES PHOTO

Is Deacon Jones roughing John Brodie, or did he trip? A tough call.
L.A. RAMS PHOTO

Deacon Jones will surely bang into Bill Munson. Another tough call.

How would you stop Merlin Olsen? Good "no call." L.A. RAMS PHOTO

It was my job to protect the health and happiness of quarterbacks. I was of little help to Sonny Jurgensen on November 26, 1967. UPI PHOTO

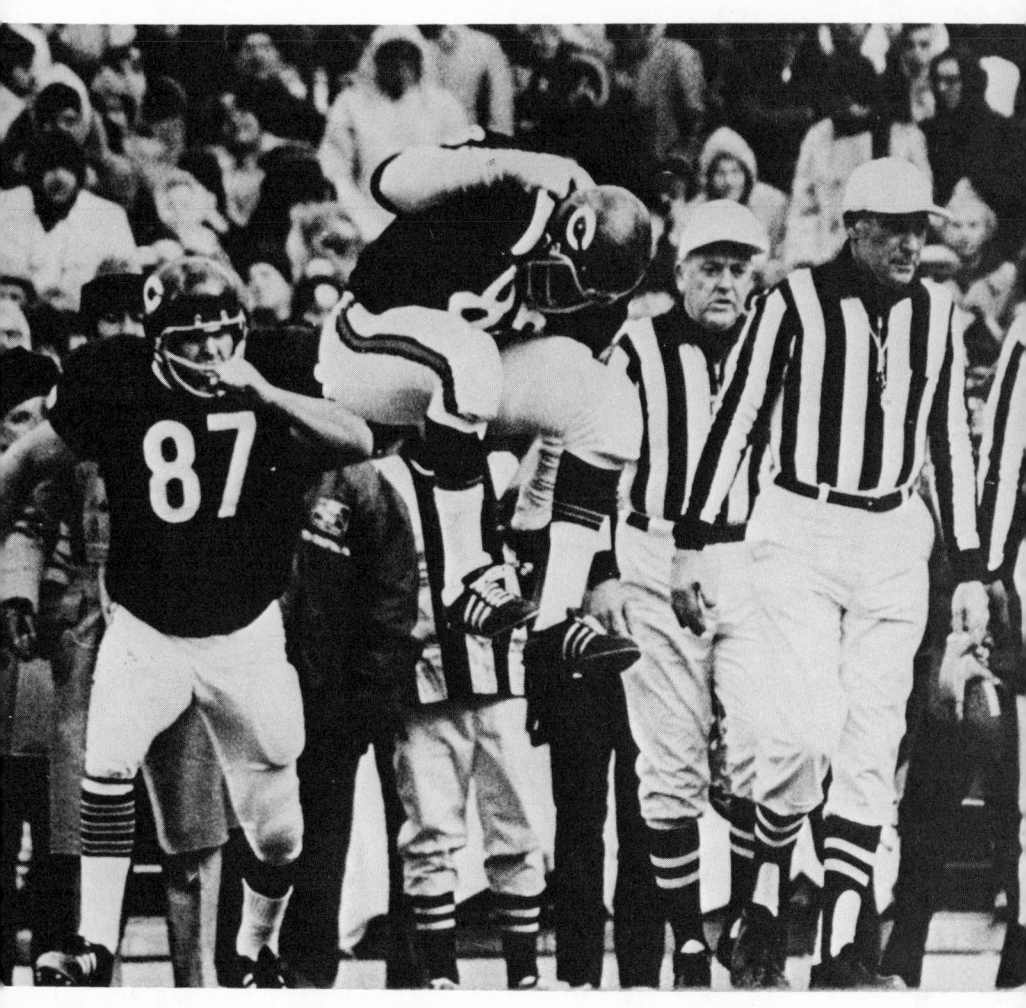

Professional football is a highly emotional game, and people get excited.
PHOTO BY BILL LANGER, CHICAGO SUN-TIMES

"You referees get to watch the game up real close. It sure looks like a fun afternoon." LOS ANGELES TIMES PHOTO

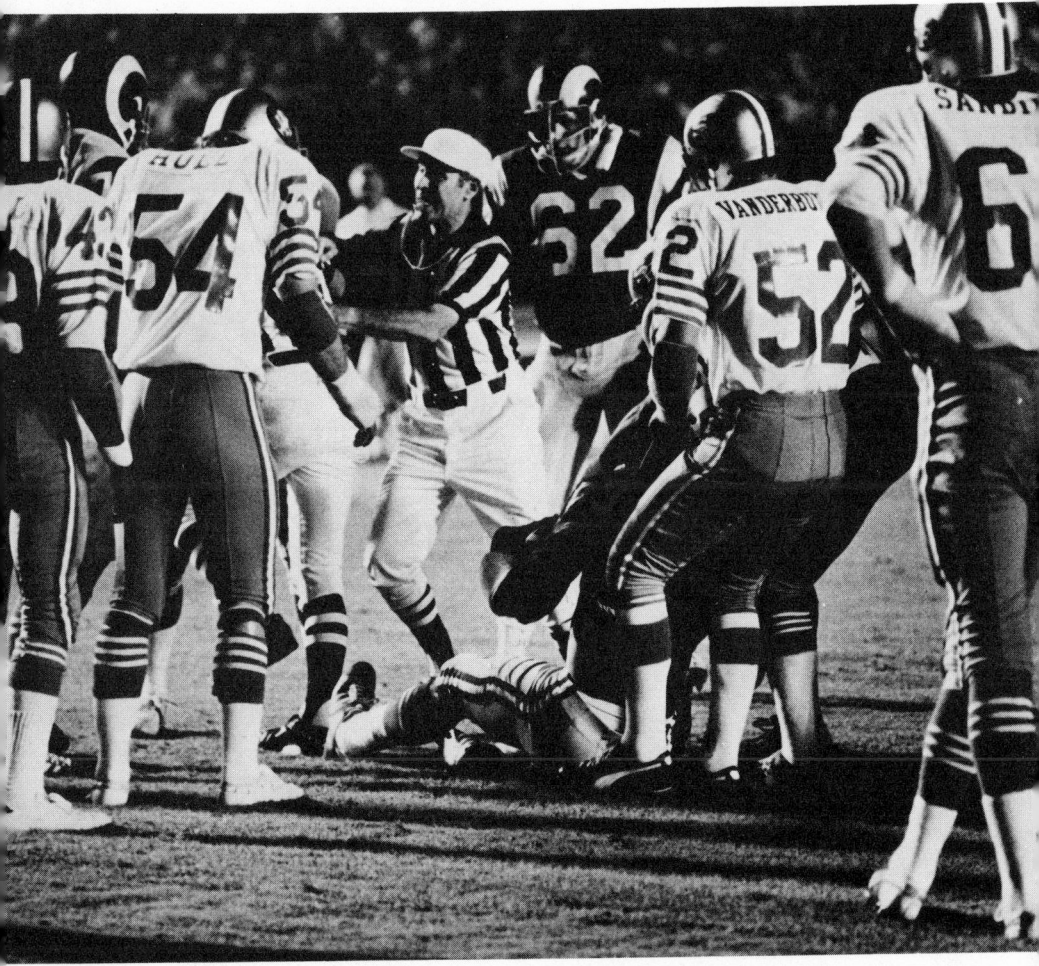

BERRY'S WORLD

"Now then — when did you first suspect you were God?"

be looking right into Tittle's eyes when Y. A. released the ball.
Tittle always went down. Hard too. The defensive player could
not change direction once he was committed and often in the air.
The only time the penalty flag flew was when there was any extra-curricular hitting. But the Giants' coaches and fans wouldn't
buy that. They always wanted a roughing-the-passer call.

In a game against Cleveland, Tittle had dropped back to pass
and couldn't get the ball away. He couldn't even throw it away.
Vince Costello, of the Browns, was all over him. Tittle ate the ball
for a 10-yard loss. Fortunately for the Giants, a Cleveland player
had held one of the Giants' ends on the scrimmage line.

At that time (the rule has since been changed for enforcement)
I measured off five yards from where Tittle went down. As I
started to walk off the five, Tittle stopped me. "Norm, you got the
wrong spot. Fouls on passing plays are from the previous spot
[spot of center snap], and not where the ball is dead. That's ten
yards downfield."

"Tittle, you're right. But that wasn't a pass play. It might have
started out as a pass play, but the ball has to be thrown. A thrown
ball is what makes a pass. Not what it started out to be."

Tittle shrugged his shoulders. He knew. Some you win, some
you lose. It's always worth a try.

Although I hear a lot of talk about roughing the quarterback,
no player can hit any other player unnecessarily out on the field.
Not where a referee can see it. Sometimes they get in a cheap
shot, but not very often. Remember that there is a ton of beef on
each side of the scrimmage line. Put that weight together, move it
around at a gallop, have them run into one another and you need
someone to keep them on the right road.

No one can hit the quarterback once he releases the ball. He
gets plenty of protection. Defensive players say he gets too much
protection. The quarterback and his coaches say he doesn't get
enough. Maybe they are right. An awful lot of quarterbacks get
hurt. There are reasons for it. Especially when they start scrambling and become runners. Very few quarterbacks get hurt if they
stay in the passing pocket. But the game has changed. Quarterbacks now run and scramble more than ever. It is a part of the offensive team's plan.

The Rules Committee is definitely committed to the policy of protecting the passer. A passer who is not standing still or fading backward is obviously out of the play after the ball has left his hand. He is to be protected until the pass ends or until he starts to move into a distinctly defensive position. The referee—and here's the judgment—must determine whether an opponent had a reasonable chance to stop his momentum during an attempt to block or bat a pass or to tackle the passer while he was still in possession of the ball. I can't expect a defensive player who is in mid-air, trying to block the pass, to change his direction as he is flying toward the quarterback. A defensive player may not strike the outstretched arm of the passer prior to or after the pass with the side of his hand or forearm.

Suppose Bert Jones, quarterback of the Baltimore Colts, drops back to pass, spots a receiver and throws the ball. Harvey Martin, the Dallas Cowboys' defensive end, comes in hard and fast and jumps up toward Jones in an attempt to block the pass. Martin is in the air, coming at Bert Jones, when Jones releases the ball. Martin doesn't have a reasonable chance to stop his momentum or drive. He runs into Jones. There is no foul, unless he brings his forearm across Jones's head or hits him something extra. We referees watch that something extra." Martin couldn't change his direction in midair, so there's no call or foul. That's a good no-call.

Let's set up the same play but with a slight variation. Jones drops back to pass, with Harvey Martin charging him in an attempt to stop the pass and to sack him. Jones gets the pass away with Martin coming toward him. Martin could veer away from Jones and avoid him as he wasn't committed in his move. His feet were still on the ground. If Martin continues on in to hit Jones, to tackle him unnecessarily or to flip him after the ball is gone, then the penalty flag is thrown. That becomes a good call. It's the small difference (and experienced judgment) that makes a no-call a foul. The defensive player, Martin in this case, has to make a reasonable attempt to minimize the contact. Or to avoid any contact when it is possible.

I remember a photograph in *Life* of Y. A. Tittle. It was a full-page shot of Tittle on his knees, his head bloody, his eyes dazed and bewildered, and his helmet on the ground, where it had rolled after it had been knocked off his head.

I remember that day well! It was the last game of that season. Pittsburgh was in Yankee Stadium, playing the Giants. Pittsburgh had to win the game. They still had a chance to win the division championship. Whichever team won that day would win the championship. That would automatically ensure them a chance to pay for the NFL title.

Pittsburgh had easily whipped the Giants earlier in the year. Very easy win. Score was 31–0. Tittle didn't play that game. He had been hurt the previous week. But he wasn't hurt that final game on December 15. The Giants had Tittle, Joe Morrison, Delbert Shofner, and Frank Gifford. Pittsburgh had a great defensive team with a tremendous pass rush. John Baker and Ernie Stautner were the defensive tackles. Both were rough, hard-nosed players.

Every time Tittle dropped back to pass, Stautner and Baker were all over him. Tittle held the ball until the last possible second. It worried me. I knew something would happen. And nobody is blamed more than the referee when the quarterback is knocked down. Neither Stautner nor Baker roughed Tittle, although they were on him, over him and breathing down his throat on most passes. Still, Tittle was having a great day.

In the fourth quarter, Tittle threw a long pass to Shofner which fell incomplete. Baker had rushed Tittle and had touched the pass just as Tittle had released the ball. He was that close to Tittle. Right on top of him. Tittle went down. Next thing I knew, Tittle was moaning, groaning and yelling, "I'm hit. They knocked my head off." His helmet was rolling on the ground and that was what he saw.

I hadn't seen the contact. I did something no experienced referee should ever do. I had peeked downfield and had not kept my eyes on the quarterback. That's dangerous, especially for the quarterback. All I could say was "No foul, Y. A. No player touched you."

Tittle stayed on his knees, his hands to his head and his eyes rolling. He told me, "Norm, if no player touched me, some Pittsburgh fan sneaked onto the field and really belted me. Or was it you?"

I knew I hadn't hit him. I didn't see any fan run onto the field. Maybe, just maybe I might have missed the call.

In that same game, Frank Gifford, now the Monday night TV commentator, made one of the greatest pass receptions I have ever seen. Tittle fell back to pass and Stautner was all over him again. Tittle barely got the ball away. Gifford was downfield about 30 yards and flew through the air in an attempt to catch the pass, which was thrown a bit away from him. Gifford extended his right hand way out while stretched out parallel to the ground. He caught the ball in his one hand. Not only did he catch it, but he held onto the ball, and brought it to his chest. Most remarkable catch I've seen in over 20 years. And I have seen hundreds of remarkable catches. Incidentally, the Giants won the game easily by a score of 31–17.

Oh, yes, just one more thing. As I left Yankee Stadium a group of kids were standing by the players' exit. We officials left through the same exit. They were waiting for Tittle and Gifford. Certainly not the referee. It was getting dark and some small youngster was holding onto his mother's hand. As I got close to them, the young boy thought I was Tittle and asked, "Can I have your autograph, Mr. Tittle?"

I looked at the kid, looked at his mother and said, "I'm not Tittle."

The woman looked at me, nodded and said, "That's all right. Sign your name anyway. My son can't read yet."

Most referees yell at the defensive players to stay away from the quarterback once he releases the ball. I always yell "Stay away from him," or "The ball is gone," or "Don't touch him." Remember, I said that a defensive player has to avoid or minimize contact with the quarterback once the ball is thrown. If the defensive player continues on and knocks the passer down, it is a 15-yard penalty and an automatic first down. If the pass is completed, we still add the 15 yards to the end of the completion. And—if a touchdown resulted from the play, we penalize the defensive team 15 yards on the next kickoff. It's expensive to rough the passer. Once again, the rule book specifically states, "Care should be exercised by the referee to ensure ample protection of the passer after the ball has left his hand. Watching or determining the flight of the pass by the referee is a secondary responsibility under these conditions."

Many, many times I never knew whether the pass was complete or incomplete. My eyes stayed with the quarterback. I never looked downfield (except when I forgot) to see what happened to the pass. Oh, if the action was clear and clean around the quarterback, then I might look downfield. It might look as if nothing is happening around the quarterback, and when you glance downfield, someone will lower the boom on the passer. I've often thought how ridiculous I would sound if I said, "Never touched him. Missed him all the way," and the quarterback had a broken jaw or leg. It gives me chills even now.

Outside of a superstar like O. J. Simpson, Gale Sayers, Hugh McElhenny or Jim Brown, the quarterback gets most of the ink from the sports writers around the country. A good one can take a team a long, long way. A poor one means a losing season no matter what else the team has. Check your winners every year. They all have outstanding quarterbacks. Look at the Super Bowl champions. It's either a Staubach, Namath, Griese, Bradshaw, Starr or Unitas. The quarterback is the man at the throttle who makes things go.

What a lot of fans don't realize is that the quarterback is the same as a runner until he throws the ball. He receives no additional protection. He can't be roughed, but then neither can any other running back or player. Protection for the quarterback starts only after the pass is made.

I remember a big tackle on the San Francisco 49ers who always came in hard after the quarterback. He was the intimidator. He would throw his forearm most of the time and miss the quarterback. But not by much. He wanted the quarterback to know he was coming and to worry about his coming and to think that maybe, just maybe he was going to get belted. Perhaps that would hurry his passes. It doesn't work out that way at all. The good quarterbacks are fearless. Once I told this tackle, #78, "Watch yourself. It'll cost you fifteen if you touch him."

As he walked by me, he nodded. On the next play his forearm came across the quarterback's helmet after the pass had been thrown. Not too hard. Enough for me to throw my flag. "That will cost you fifteen, Number Seventy-eight," I told him.

He looked at me and replied, "It was worth it."

Was he ever wrong. San Francisco intercepted the pass and ran it back for a touchdown. I took the score away, but actually it was #78 who took the score away for his team. I gave the ball back to Detroit, tacked on 15 yards and signaled a first down. Number 78 watched me walk off the 15 yards. Then he yelled, "I never touched him." Detroit then went in for a score. That's why the good ones hate to foul.

After a referee has been scorched a time or two, he learns never to answer a screaming coach on the sideline. That's always the best policy, especially when he is upset about a call. If he wants to take a time-out to discuss the call, fine. If he wants me to stop the game in order to go over to hear him scream at me, no way. This time it happened in Oakland. Things weren't going just right for the Raiders. At least that's what Coach Madden thought. He always thought that when they were behind. He was letting me know he was displeased. Isn't that a nice way to say it?

On this particular play, Stabler, Oakland's quarterback, was thrown for a large loss. Joe Greene, of Pittsburgh, had really barreled in and flipped Stabler. Legal all the way. Madden didn't believe anyone could get in that quickly. Not unless he beat the snap.

There wasn't a flag on the play. There wasn't anything illegal about the play. It just was a helluva move by Joe Greene. Madden kept yelling at me. "Norm, wasn't Greene off side? I want to know. Why wasn't the flag thrown? Answer me, damn it. Talk to me."

I didn't answer. Finally, Madden yelled, "Okay, Norm. Don't answer me. Just shake your head one way or another, and we'll be able to hear you."

Never a dull moment working an Oakland game.

I vividly remember a championship game between the Baltimore Colts and the Green Bay Packers that had quarterback problems. Really had them. The Colts had lost Johnny Unitas three weeks before the season ended. His backup replacement, Gary Cuozzo, was injured the week before the championship game. He was also out for the remainder of the year. Coach Don Shula converted Tom Matte, a running back, into an instant quarterback for the game that meant the whole ball of wax.

The real quarterback story of that game was what happened to Bart Starr, the Packers' quarterback. Starr lasted one play. On the first play of the game, he threw a forward pass which was completed to the Packers' 25-yard line. The receiver who caught the ball got tackled and fumbled the ball. Don Shinnick, an excellent

Colt linebacker, picked up the ball and started to run toward the Packers' goal line. Starr tried to tackle Shinnick, but was blocked by one of Shinnick's teammates. Starr went down and out for the afternoon. That brought in Zeke Bratkowski, the Packers' backup quarterback. Zeke was an old pro and had been around, but he wasn't a Bart Starr, even in his best days. But he kept the Packers in the ball game. He hung in there and was doing a great job. Later on in the fourth quarter Bratkowski dropped back to pass, but never passed the ball. Billy Ray Smith, an aggressive defensive tackle, came in very tough and hit Bratkowski with his hand in a swinging motion around Bratkowski's head. He went down like a chopped tree. I thought he had been shot. In fact, I thought he was dead. He still held onto the ball. How he kept it, I never will know.

My flag went down immediately. Some people thought I had signaled a roughing-the-passer call. It wasn't. The pass was never thrown, so it couldn't be roughing the passer. It was a personal foul. All players are prohibited from striking, swinging at or clubbing another player on the head, neck or face with the heel, back side of the hand, wrist, forearm, elbow or clasped hands. It is a 15-yard penalty and automatic first down. It wasn't of a vicious or flagrant nature in my view. If it were, I would have run Smith. It was a bang-bang play and reaction.

Coach Don Shula was screaming at me. He was the coach of the Colts then. Shula knows the rules, understands officiating problems and is on the Competition Committee, the NFL's rule-making body. And he knows how to win. Time was out. Bratkowski was out. And I walked over to Coach Shula, who was yelling for me to come see him.

"Norm, it's not a foul. He's not the quarterback. He's a runner. You can do anything to a runner," Shula shouted.

I yelled back, "You can't hit any player—runner, quarterback, anyone—in the head in a swinging, clubbing way. It's a foul. In fact, Zeke may be dead."

Finally, Bratkowski stirred, moved, and was helped to his feet. After a time-out he continued. The game went on and on. That was the game that ended in a 10–10 tie, when Don Chandler, the Packers' field goal kicker, made his controversial field goal which the Baltimore Colts protested and protested. It didn't help them any, for the game went into overtime. After 13 minutes and 33 seconds of overtime play, Chandler kicked a 25-yard field goal for the winning score. Clean through the uprights. No question or discussion on that one. That was the longest game ever played in the NFL up to that time.

John Brodie, who is now the color man on the NBC broadcasts, is as good at that as he was in throwing the ball for the 49ers. Always a gentleman. I liked John Brodie as a player. He enjoyed a laugh, even at his own expense. But he didn't let that get in the way of working the officials for whatever breaks he could get.

San Francisco was playing the Chicago Bears in Wrigley Field, Chicago. Dick Butkus, the great middle linebacker for the Bears and probably the best middle linebacker that I have ever seen, was having himself an afternoon. Even more so than the usual Butkus game. He was truly outstanding. That's something to behold, believe me.

Every time Brodie faded back to pass, Butkus was all over him. He sacked him, trapped him and bowled him over constantly after he had released the ball. It was close to roughing the passer, but not quite. "Not quite" kept the penalty flag in my pocket. In the fourth quarter Brodie was really belted. Legally though. I felt for him. Brodie jumped up and ran after me. "Norm," he shouted, "Butkus is killing me. I'm bruised. I'm hurting. I'm dying. I'm starting to get Butkus-shy. I can't stand to see him coming at me. Can't you see him banging me?"

I listened to Brodie. I said, "John, why don't you do what I'm doing? When Butkus gets close to you, I just close my eyes. I can't stand it either."

It was the first time Brodie was speechless that day. Then a big grin covered his face. He was class. Still is.

When he was the Oakland coach, John Madden would tell anyone willing to listen, "It's idiotic to give the kicker so much protection and the quarterback so little. No one can brush a kicker when the ball is kicked, but you sure as hell can knock the quarterback on his ass." Coach Madden wanted to have the referee blow a horn once the quarterback released the ball. After that horn no one could touch the quarterback. That would keep the passer healthy. Madden may have had something there, but I got enough advice from him about what I could do with my whistle.

How about the running-into-the-kicker call? Does a kicker have too much protection? I don't think so. All I know is that the referee is on the spot. Hours and hours are spent practicing techniques for blocking the kick. It isn't by chance that a kick is blocked. Each defensive man has definite responsibilities. Some blitz, some pull the offensive guard aside so his teammate can shoot the gap (illegal), some jump over linemen, some stand on their teammates (illegal), some overload on one side to get an advantage, and some knock the center who is snapping the ball right back on his keester. Add it all up and it's tough on a referee. Especially if the kicker falls to the ground. That seems to be a signal for coaches, players and fans to start the chant "Running into the kicker, running into the kicker." It isn't the five-yard penalty they want. It's that automatic first down that goes with it. The kicker's team gets to keep the ball. Worse yet, it always seems to work out that they then go on to score. That compounds the judgment call. The officials catch hell from the other team's coaches and players.

There are keys referees use. The rule book spells them out. Unfortunately, the rule book doesn't spell out judgment, and that's what makes the job so different. A kicker usually lines up 14 yards behind the center. That distance from the scrimmage line gives just about the right time to get a kick away. No more and no less. A poor snap from center or an extra step by the kicker means a blocked kick. In the excitement of a game it is amazing how many kickers who know better will take the first step with the wrong foot—the kicking foot. Especially as most of them line up the 14 yards behind the center.

The primary responsibility for avoiding the kicker rests with the onrushing lineman if he does not touch the ball. Some of the more experienced kickers in the League should belong to the Screen Actors Guild. They put on an Academy Award performance every time a defensive player gets close enough to block the kick. The punter then twists and groans as he falls to the ground. All with grimaces and ohs and ahs. It's quite theatrical, very dramatic. Raises hell with the referee. The crowd, coaches and teammates start the refrain "Running into the kicker." Like hell it is. It is a referee's job to see that no one gets away with that act. I yell at the kicker, "Get up off your ass. You weren't even hit. Stop trying to make me look bad."

The kicker couldn't care less. He tells me, "Make you look bad?

How could I do that now? You've been that way for years." They smile though when they say that.

Some blockers get very cute at rolling an onrushing opponent into the kicker. It doesn't take too much of a turn on a moving man to change the direction of the player. Right smack into the kicker. Though the defensive man bumps the kicker, it is the result of the block. That isn't running into the kicker. But that doesn't stop the crowd from roaring. The team plays percentage football. Sometimes it draws the foul. It's wishful thinking. It's an easy call. The referee has no one else to watch. He gets a good look at the play. All the way.

Sometimes, just sometimes, the referee forgets to get that good look. He takes a peek downfield to see if the field goal is good or not. I was in Detroit one Sunday afternoon. Errol Mann was the field goal specialist for the Lions that year. He made the field goal and I signaled good. I didn't see the storming players run all over Mann. They really must have belted him. Mann screamed, "Shit. Where's your damn flag? They killed me."

I looked back toward him, saw Mann on the ground sprawled six different ways. "Never laid a hand on you. Field goal is good. Get up."

During the week I received eleven letters from Detroit friends. Friends? Each letter had a cartoon with the kicker with his head buried in the ground to the waist, with his feet sticking straight up in the air. The caption read, "Never touched him."

A few years ago I was working in Shea Stadium, home of the New York Jets. It was a Saturday afternoon televised game against Miami in New York. Miami was winning everything. Not that day though. Nothing came easy for them. Namath had one of his days. He picked the teeth out of the defensive secondary.

Late in the first half Miami had its first good field position. The Jets were forced to kick from their own 10-yard line. Greg Gantt, the punter, dropped back into his own end zone and booted the ball. Just as the ball left his foot and was on its way, Mike Kolen, of Miami, blitzed and almost blocked the kick. He came in at a slight angle. One of the Jets' blockers barely brushed Kolen as he stormed in. Kolen went through the blocker as if he weren't there. It didn't change Kolen's direction or speed. He ran into the kicker and brushed him enough to fall down. Gantt fell to the ground, squirmed and groaned. It was worth an Academy Award. Best bit of acting all day.

I didn't need that kind of help. It looked like a con job. It really was running into the kicker so the act was wasted. I threw my flag. That was worth five yards and a first down for the Jets. It gave the Jets the ball again—and good-bye to field position for Miami.

Coach Don Shula was beside himself. I walked over and let him play the role of the irate coach. Only thing was that he wasn't playing. He said, "Tell me, Norm, how am I going to coach my players if you call that running into the kicker? I tell them to avoid the kicker. My man was blocked into the punter. What can I tell my players? How can I coach them? What should I tell them?"

I listened, looked at Shula and answered, "Coach, keep telling them what you've been telling them all season. Keep coaching them the way you have all season. You have a helluva record. I wouldn't change a thing."

Shula looked at me, winked, and walked away.

As so often happens, the situation occurred again when the Dolphins had to punt soon after. This time a Jet player did the same thing Kolen had done for Miami. Same play. Same penalty. This time I heard Shula yelling, "Great call. That's watching them all the way." Weeb Ewbank, the Jets' coach, was screaming exactly what Shula had screamed previously. "Keep your eyes open. Blocked into the kicker." It all depends what happens to your side.

The strangest play from kick formation that I have ever seen happened in St. Louis. Danny Villanueva, the Dallas kicker at that time, was back in punt formation. It was late in the fourth quarter, fourth down and 20 yards to go for Dallas. Villanueva punted the ball. No St. Louis player crossed the scrimmage line to block the punt or to keep the kicker honest. All of them turned their backs to the punter and ran downfield. It was their intention to form a picket line for the receiver and pick up some long yardage on the return. There was only one problem. Villanueva didn't punt the ball.

Villanueva took one step forward, stopped and couldn't believe what was happening. No one was rushing him. In fact, no one was

around him. That is, no one but me. And I wasn't about to block
the kick. Danny looked at me with one of those "Where the hell
are they?" looks. I didn't look back. I was afraid that I would
laugh aloud. That would look bush. I held my spot. But not Villanueva. He took off and ran toward the St. Louis sideline. He ran
along the inside of the line. Charley Winner, the St. Louis coach,
was going bananas. He ran alongside of Villanueva, though he
stayed on the outside of the sideline. With every step he took, he
yelled, "Hey, you stupid bastards, turn around, turn around." As
he kept running, "bastards" turned to "sonavabitches" and finally
to the more serious dirty words.

No one turned around, and Coach Winner was out of his mind.
Finally, after 30 yards one of his players heard him. He forced
Villanueva out of bounds after a 35-yard gain. It was at the right
time too, for Coach Winner was starting to repeat himself. I didn't
blame Winner. Danny's run, not punt, turned the game around.
When the gun sounded, Winner was still running that sideline.
Much slower, though. And talking to himself.

Professional football is a game of inches. Any advantage a team
can get counts in the win column. That's why coaches spend so
much time on the little things. They add up. Strategy counts. Mo-
tivation and an understanding of what the coach means are most
important. Especially in the kicking game.

Don Cockroft dropped back into punt formation. The ball was
snapped to him, and he took his initial step forward as if to punt.
But he ran with the ball. And made a first down. I looked over to
their bench. Coach Nick Skorich was smiling.

After the game, which Cleveland eventually won, a reporter
asked Skorich if the fake punt and run was a planned play. I
never have forgotten Skorich's words. "I guess so. The kicker decides whether to run or punt. My only suggestion is that if he does
decide to run, he better damn well make it."

Coaches learn from each other. It doesn't take long for the word
to spread. Remember Errol Mann getting knocked down on the
field goal which was good? We automatically assumed the three
points would stand. Coach Weeb Ewbank changed the routine
decision to an option. The option was always there, but I never
thought of it. I just signaled good. Three points are three points. A

bird in the hand or something. Three points were added to the scoreboard. Television went for the commercial. Cut and dried, right? Wrong.

Back we go to Baltimore again. It was the Packers and the Colts. Both needed the win. It always seemed that way. It was the third quarter. The game was shaping up like the usual Packers-Colts affair. It was fourth down around the Packers' nine-yard line with not quite five yards to go for a first down. The field goal team ran onto the field. Green Bay jumped off side at the snap. But Lou Michaels kicked the field goal. I didn't pay any attention to the Packers' offside penalty. I knew the Colts would take the three points. They had already added it to the scoreboard. I pointed to the television man to take his commercial. No one said anything. Both teams left the field and in came the kicking and receiving teams for the kickoff. Not quite. Gino Marchetti, the Colts' defensive captain, ran up to me. He was a smart one. Thinking all the time. "Norm," asked Gino, "don't we get an option on that play? Can't we turn the penalty down if we made the first down?"

Slowly, slowly, I nodded. "Yes, Gino, you get an option. It's a first down if it's there. It's not automatic. You've got to get the necessary yardage." I hoped he would run off the field and say, "We'll take the three points." Not Gino.

"Measure it, Norm. Let's see if we made the first down."

The head linesman had moved the stakes. Once the signal had been given and the teams left the field, he moved the chains. Now we had a problem. Where did the play start from? How much did they need for a first down? I asked Ed Marion, the head linesman, "Ed, where did we start from on that play? Do you have the spot?"

Ed looked serious, but his eyes were dancing. He was enjoying my problem. "You have a problem, Norm. The chains and box marker were moved on your signal. I think it was somewhere around the nine-yard line. Either side of it."

"Around the nine-yard line. Either side of it." I had a problem. I knew it would be very tight. I went over to the sideline, picked up the phone to the press box and got the play-by-play statistician. "Where did the play start from? What yard line was the ball on?"

The statistician answered, "Around the nine-yard line." All the time Coach Lombardi was screaming into my ear. He was yelling and shouting. I ignored the coach, for he wasn't helping. All he wanted was his fair advantage. I said over the phone, "Right on the nine-yard line. Great. That's a definite spot." I wasn't about to say "around" with Lombardi at my shoulder.

I walked over to the nine-yard line, asked for the ball and started to measure off the penalty. Unitas and Marchetti watched for the Colts, and Willie Davis and Bart Starr watched for the Packers. They measured my steps carefully. Television was missing it all. They were on a commercial. They caught the tail end of my act. I stood on the nine-yard line and said aloud to the captains, "Half the distance to the goal line brings the ball to the four-and-a-half-yard line. Bring out the chains. Let's measure it."

Fortunately, we had that spot. The chain crew had written down where the first down had started. They brought the chains out. They were about a foot short of the first down. I took a deep breath of relief. I was off the hook. The Colts would take the sure three points. Unitas looked over to the bench and saw Ewbank give the go-ahead signal. Unitas told me, "We'll go for it."

Lenny Moore took a hand-off from Unitas and scored standing up. Six points and the try point gave them seven big points instead of the three from the field goal. The place went wild. Not quite as wild as Lombardi. He was questioning the "nine-yard spot." I was lucky. Just think if Lenny Moore had made only a foot or so and I had had to give the Colts a first down from a lost spot. I still would be in Baltimore.

We changed our mechanics. Now if there is a foul on a score, we hold our signal until we give the options. Television holds and doesn't leave the game until the referee makes the decision.

Pass interference is a problem. Not in the official's mind, but for the official. Everyone around the country sees it differently. It is really a matter of knowing what to look for. Fans see what they want to see. And if it's against their team, then it's wrong—the officials blew it—again. Most people forget that both teams have a right to the path of the ball. Any bodily contact, however severe, between two players who are making a simultaneous and bona fide attempt to catch the ball is not interference. Reads easy, doesn't it? Sounds even easier. It's a helluva call. Nothing but trouble, but it is a call that has to be made. That's what they are paying us for. The official on the play has to interpret what a bona fide attempt is. It certainly isn't a little push, a slight nudge or a half-ass bump some defenders use in going for the ball. It's a real bang-bang play. Sometimes it is a 50- or 60-yard penalty, for the ball is placed where the foul happened.

All pro quarterbacks can throw the long bomb. If a defensive player is beat on the play, he will push, shove or grab his man because his opponent will catch the ball anyway. Why not take a chance? If the foul is called, start screaming at that blind Tom, "I was playing the ball, you half-ass ref. What the hell are you watching? It was clean all the way. I've got as much right to the ball as he has. Don't you know that? How long have you been working? You homer."

Every gesture, every word and every action by the player bring forth thunderous boos. And that's not even what the coaches are yelling. Any pass interference call is clear-cut in the official's eye or he wouldn't call it. It's not a call to guess on. It most often means the ball game. By the time the fouler stops reacting, it becomes a questionable call in the minds of the spectators. Mistakes are made, of course, but the percentage missed on this type of call is infinitesimal. Every argument is for that fair advantage. If not on that play, then for the next one.

It takes guts to call a long defensive pass interference. Especially in the end zone. That puts the ball on the one-yard line with four downs to get the touchdown. No way is a coach going to believe the foul was there. Especially when the player involved claims he never fouled. No one ever fouls. That's what they say. Just try having a football game without officials. See what would happen. The stretcher concession would bring a high price. It would be mayhem out on the field.

Once in Cleveland our crew had a foul-free game until the last play. I thought we were going to get into the record book. I can't ever remember a game in my 22 years that didn't have a foul called. In this game there were no fouls. Unbelievable. On the last play of the game, a fight broke out. It was the damnedest thing I ever saw. Players were pairing off as if they were going to dance. Some did, I guess. There were other small groups rolling on the ground. It's hard to hurt one another with all that equipment on. Watch the next fight during a game. Notice how no player ever takes his helmet off, even if he needs a thing to swing. He will not leave himself unprotected.

I stood back from the melee. I had my pencil and paper out. I was taking numbers. It was safer from that position. Herm Rohrig was with me, keeping me company, and he also had his pencil out. There we were in the center of the field, watching the fight. A referee will step in and stop a fight if he can catch it at its inception. That's to prevent it from spreading. Once a fight starts and blows (not words) are exchanged, stand back and watch. When it is all over, get the two players who started the whole damn thing and run them out of the game. No strain, no pain if you are lucky. I turned to Rohrig (now the Big Ten supervisor of officials) and said, "Herm, did you have Number Forty-seven and Number Seventy-eight fighting?"

Herm looked straight ahead and replied, "That's right, Norm. That's what I saw. Those two guys are gone. I guess so is our record-breaking no-foul game. That's gone too." It took 18 minutes to replay the last play. And I missed my plane.

In 1947 the NFL added a fifth official. In 1965 they added a sixth official. In 1978 they added a seventh official. It has helped. But you need 22 officials out on the field, one to keep an eye on each player. And that's no assurance of a foul-free game.

When the League decided to add the sixth official in 1965, Mark Duncan, then Supervisor of Officials, called me. "How about a duty statement for the sixth official?"

What Duncan meant: "What the hell should he do, where should he stand, and what should we call him?"

The Competition Committee, the official rules body of the League, knew what they wanted. They wanted the new official, the sixth official, to stand across from the head linesman on the scrimmage line. Two things were required of the new official. First, to clear up the confusion on the quick backward or forward pass that is close. Second, to get a good look at the new breed of quarterback who scrambles all over the field and then decides to throw. Make sure he is behind the line when he throws the ball. If the ball is thrown beyond the line of scrimmage, it is a foul. Call it.

During any game in any given week the quarterback drops back two or three yards after he takes the snap from his center. He then throws a quick, short swing pass behind the scrimmage line to one of his backs. If no one catches the ball and the ball hits the ground, that's when all hell breaks loose. If the pass goes forward and falls to the ground, it's a simple incomplete pass play. No player can recover it. It becomes a dead ball. Play is over. Everything stops. However, if the swing pass goes backward (or laterally) and hits the ground, it's a free ball. It's alive. The defensive players may recover the ball and keep it. A tough call when it's tight—a foot or so either way. The sixth official's job is to watch the ball on a swing pass. If it's backward, watch the official raise his arm straight out from the shoulder. That alerts all the other officials that the ball is alive and they must keep on their toes.

George Halas, coach of the Bears, always had a routine he went through with me before each game. He wanted all those short swing passes that were almost lateral to be called forward passes. Then if it was close, and it was backward, and the ball was alive, he wanted to structure the referee to call it an incomplete pass. Here's the way the conversation went.

"Hi, Norm. It's good to see you. Always like to have you work our games. You know we throw that swing pass. It's always a forward pass. We don't have a backward pass play in any way. We're not foolish to take that chance. Be sure to give it a good look. Just remember that it's a forward pass play. We don't have a swing backward pass play in our play book."

He always had a card to illustrate what he meant. I knew what he was saying. I always gave him my serious look and always answered, "Coach, if it goes forward, it's a forward pass. If it goes backward or lateral, it's a backward pass. It all depends on how it goes. I'll give it a real good look." By this time the other team's coach was rushing up to hear what the hell was being said.

When the decision to add the sixth official was made, there was some discussion on what to call him. We knew the official would watch the swing pass. We also knew that he would watch the scrambling quarterback to get the correct spot when he released the ball near the scrimmage line. It made a difference. A big difference. If the quarterback threw a forward pass after he had crossed the scrimmage line, it was a loss of a down and a five-yard penalty. One of the three combination penalties in the rule book. The referee was having a problem getting the right spot whenever he was blocked out of the way.

Duncan wanted me to work up a job responsibility for the new official. He had his own ideas, coaches had submitted their views, and now he wanted to get a referee's thoughts. He got it. The job responsibility was worked out to everyone's satisfaction. Now we had to select a name for the new official. What were we going to call him? We got all kinds of suggestions. Names like side judge, stationary judge, back judge #2, line judge and others were tossed into the hat. It was finally decided to call him line judge.

Mark Duncan had the last word. He said, "What's the difference what name we give him? Once the game starts, they'll call him a blind sonavabitch."

Another tough call is a pass completion near the sideline. In pro football the receiver has to have both feet in bounds (on the field) to make it a legal completed pass. If a receiver is close to the sideline when he catches a forward pass, he will drag that second foot to get it in bounds. The pro rule differs from the amateur rule. In college and high school football the receiver of a forward pass needs to land with only one foot in bounds. That throws many fans off and brings on the noise.

Take a look at the receivers in the NFL who have been around the League for some while. Watch Cliff Branch of Oakland, Rick Upchurch of Denver, Ahmad Rashad of the Vikings, Preston Pearson and Tony Hill of the Cowboys, Steve Largent of Seattle, Lynn Swann and Johnny Stallworth of the Steelers, John Jefferson of San Diego and Joe Washington of the Colts. Hell, look at all receivers close to the sideline. Watch their feet. That's what makes it a tough call. The official on the play has to watch the receiver's feet to see if both of them land in bounds; watch to see the player catch the ball; and then watch to see if he is pushed out of bounds while in the air. The official then has to decide whether the player would have landed in the field of play with both feet in bounds if he wasn't pushed out of bounds while in the air after the catch. It's a bang-bang. The old pros—Fears, Hirsch and Ray Berry (who was the best at it)—practiced hours perfecting the one-two step on the sideline. The good ones still do. Hours and hours and hours.

I remember the hell we caught on a sideline pass play. At least George Murphy, an excellent head linesman, did. It was in the championship game between the Baltimore Colts at Cleveland against the Browns. Unitas dropped back on one play, threw deep to his end, Jimmy Orr, who was streaking downfield in bounds near the sideline. I remember peeking downfield, as no one was near Unitas at that time. I saw Orr, whose back was to me as he ran toward the Browns' goal line. He caught the ball over his shoulder and ran a few yards in bounds and then ran out of bounds as he was being closely chased. At least that's what I thought I saw. I saw George Murphy, the official right on the play, signal "no good" by crossing his arms across his chest. I couldn't believe it. I noticed that no one on the Colts' bench (right near the play) raised too much fuss. The television cameras replayed the play and the announcers said, "The head linesman blew the call. Take a look and see Orr catch the ball." They showed it from three different angles.

Several months later we got a fourth-angle look at the play from an end-line camera shooting up from the end zone. It showed very clearly that Jimmy Orr never caught the ball. He was juggling it as he went off the field. Great call. But Murphy caught hell the next day as no one saw the shot we saw months later. The rule states that the player has to have complete control of the ball before it is considered complete and caught. That also adds an extra dimension to the one-two step on the sideline. The official has to watch the catch, watch the feet to see that they are in bounds, watch the ball and watch the sideline. In spite of what you hear, officials have two eyes.

When I mention two eyes I can't help but think of a game between the Bears and San Francisco in Kezar Stadium, the old ball park of the 49ers. In recent years linebackers have become as well known to the average fan as the highly publicized quarterbacks. Sports writers and television commentators have realized how important this position is in the total picture of winning. The linebacker is a natural to spot. His position behind the defensive line is flexible enough for him to make many tackles and key interceptions. He is where the action is. He usually is at the bottom of every pileup. Without a top linebacker, it is almost impossible to go all the way or to be a top contender. It started with Huff, Schmidt, Nitschke and George and continued with Lanier, Bergey, Butkus and Lee Roy Jordon. Check your winners and see what I mean. Every single one of them and all the others in the League are nimble-witted and salty.

One of my favorites was Dick Butkus. In a game between the

49ers and the Bears the players were really going at it. It was a rainy day and the field in Kezar was muddy. John Brodie, the 49er quarterback, faked a pass and then handed the ball to the fullback on the draw play. It went for long yardage before Butkus moved over a few players to catch up with the runner. Somehow and somewhere along the way a mud clod went into Butkus' right eye. It literally blacked him out. As the doctor worked over him and helped relieve the pain, I stood nearby and watched them clean his eye. As Butkus jumped up to leave the field, I said, "Thought you'd lost that eye. What would you do then?"

Butkus didn't even break his stride as he ran by me. He yelled back, "If I lost my eye, I would become a referee. One eye is more than I would need from what I've seen out here today."

Whenever you see the referee signal an infraction of the rules by grabbing his own wrist, that's holding. And it is usually an easy call. What we call a run-of-the-mill foul. Judgment is so important. If it affects the outcome of the play, *bang!* goes the flag. On a running play if it is away from the point of attack (where the play is going), we give it a hard second look. Neither the offensive team nor the defensive team can hold. Most offensive holding occurs on pass plays where the linemen and backs use their hands illegally in blocking. They are trying to protect their quarterback from getting sacked and thrown for a loss. These players can't hold a defensive man by grabbing his shirt, pulling him down or tackling him.

A defensive player may tackle the man with the ball. A defensive man may not hold any opponent other than a runner.

The obvious and run-of-the-mill fouls are no problems. It's the unusual and seldom-seen ones that create confusion—and discussion. Such a foul was called against the New York Giants years ago when I was working in Yankee Stadium one Sunday afternoon. Andy Robustelli was the team's defensive captain. He came up to hear the explanation of the foul. He didn't like the explanation and didn't like the penalty. Robustelli was a great competitor and he also knew the rules. He was thinking all the time on the field. He didn't hesitate to tell me what he thought of the call. As I was walking off the yardage, he walked with me and complained on every step. Just as I had finished my 15-yard walk, I turned to him and said, "Andy, it's a rule."

"Well, then, it's a helluva rule," he complained.

That should have ended the conversation. As he was walking away, I said, "Look, I don't write the rule book."

Sam Huff, a favorite of mine and a great linebacker for the Giants, had been walking with Andy and me and listening. He stopped, turned to me and said, "Yeah, but you could at least read it once in a while."

I didn't smile though I thought it was funny. But then Sam went on, "Come to think of it, if you read it, it would have to be written in Braille."

Howard Buttery, a very good and close friend of mine, is an avid sports fan. Over a period of years he has lost his eyesight and is now blind. However, he follows all sports and knows everything that is happening in the sports world. He still goes to the ball games as he likes to feel the game even if he can't see it. He takes his transistor radio with him and it seems to work out just fine.

At the end of a tough Los Angeles Rams game with Minnesota, I met Howard and his wife with others for dinner and we discussed the game. One of the wives (not mine) questioned a controversial call that I had made in the game. It had stopped the game. The boos did, not me.

Before I could answer, my blind friend Howard piped up, "Norm was right, that was the way I saw it."

That was just the kind of assurance I needed.

Remember Joe Muha? He was a great offensive and defensive player for the Philadelphia Eagles during their championship years. He later joined my crew as the umpire. That's the official right behind the defensive line who keeps an eye or two open for holding. That's where a lot of holding takes place. The players hold to give their quarterback more time to throw or they hold to spring a running back clear of the line. Anyway, Muha was a good umpire. Many former players become umpires if they become officials in the League, men like Pat Harder, Gerry Hart, Frank Sinkovitz, Lou Palazzi and several others. They need to be big physically for that position.

An umpire's primary function is to prevent holding by the interior linemen. By preventing it, I mean he has to watch for it and to call it foul. That's the best preventive officiating there is.

One hectic afternoon in St. Louis a number of the defensive linemen were screaming, "The're holding me, they're holding me!"

As we were leaving the field at the end of the first half, the defensive line coach of the Cardinals, who had played ball with Muha in Philadelphia, complained bitterly to me about the holding.

I told him, "Listen, Muha is right on the play every time. He's looking for it. That's his job. He'd call it if he saw it."

The coach threw up his hands, turned aside and shouted, "He'll never call it. He held all the time when he was a player, even in warm-up drills in practice. He thinks it's legal."

Muha grinned when I told him about it later in the locker room.

Frank Varrichione, a hard-nosed tackle for the Rams, was often called for holding. Especially by Muha. When Muha's flag was thrown and the play was over, I would walk up to Muha and say, "Whatcha got, Joe?" I knew but I asked.

Muha would point to his flag, "Holding on Number Seventy of the Rams. Right at that spot. Grabbed the guy's shirt and almost ripped it off his back."

I walked off the yardage, listened to the bleeps from the Rams' coaches. "You're picking on him. Never laid a hand on him. Give it a good look, damn it."

A year later we had the Rams again. This time in Cleveland and it was anybody's ball game. Close. Very close. Muha threw his flag on a completed pass play by the Rams. Back came the long completed pass. The gain was wiped out. And a penalty walked off against the Rams. I walked over to Muha. "Who was it, Joe? What was it?"

Joe stood over his flag, turned to me and pointed. "I didn't get the whole number. It started with a seven. Must have been Number Seventy."

The coaches were screaming, "Who was the foul on? Who was it on?"

Muha yelled back, "Seventy."

I thought George Allen, the Rams' new head coach at the time, would go off his rocker. His offensive assistant coach yelled at Muha, "Hey, Muha, Number Seventy quit at the end of last season. He's not with the club anymore. We don't even have a Number Seventy on the squad. You always picked on him."

Muha was close. It was Number Seventy-nine who had held. It really didn't matter whether it was #70 or #79. Just as long as the foul was there. Muha didn't miss many. He never guessed. As a former player, he was especially conscious of the ways in which holding could change the outcome of a game. He just wouldn't allow anyone to get away with it.

When I speak of holding, I immediately think of Deacon Jones, the great defensive end of the Los Angeles Rams. People talk of great players. Give me a half dozen Deacon Joneses and I'll play anybody. Whenever Deacon was in the ball game, and he wasn't around the quarterback, I'd look to see who was holding him. He just couldn't be contained for too many plays. His sack total of quarterbacks was tops in the League for many years. I didn't need any film to see why he was not near the quarterback sometimes. He was so quick, so tough, and so good that an offensive tackle had to hold a little bit.

Deacon was an outstanding defensive end and the originator of the two-handed slap to the head. Head-slapping is what we called it—legal when he was in his prime. They had to change the rules to slow him down. Prior to the rule change Jones would hit the offensive tackle on the head with his left hand and as the tackle's head was moving to the other side, he would come across and hit him with his right hand. Open palm, of course, which was legal. Now a player can only use his open palm on the scrimmage line if he is being blocked. And only one hand and one time. No more head-slapping. That took care of Deacon Jones. He wasn't any offensive tackle. If he had stayed, he would have adjusted, quickly too. I often told Deacon jokingly, "If they didn't allow the head slap, you wouldn't have seen the big city."

I remember one day in Washington, D.C., when the Rams were playing the Redskins. Deacon was having one of his better days. No one could contain him. He was all over the quarterback. Finally, #77, a good offensive tackle on the Redskins, grabbed Jones as he came charging in. I threw my flag and yelled, "Number Seventy-seven, you're holding him."

Number 77 looked at me in disgust, and replied, "How in hell would you play him?"

After a number of years in this business, a referee knows just about everyone in professional football. We know which players are the talkers, which players are headhunters, and which coaches are the needlers. A clever and quick needle keeps a referee on his toes.

An experienced referee can tell when a player is reaching the end of the playing line. We say that he loses it in his legs and gets more active with his mouth. One of my favorite all-time defensive tackles was Daddy Lipscomb. He was delightful. Never a problem. Always did a full day's work and had a good time doing it. I liked him as a person, and I think everyone appreciated the effort he expended on the field. I don't ever remember him taking a cheap shot at anyone.

He had a wonderful routine going when he was at his peak. There were times when no one, and I mean no one, could keep him from getting the quarterback. After downing the quarterback for a big loss, he would always offer to help him back on his feet with a little advice. "Don't try to get away from Big Daddy. I want to be your friend."

It was during one of his last games that he kept complaining that he was being held. He kept after me to remind me that they were holding him. Finally, I looked up at him and said, "Daddy, they didn't hold you five years ago."

He looked down at me, grinned and went back to his position.

Do you remember Leo Nomellini? He was a unanimous All-American when he was at the University of Minnesota, and an All-Pro when he was with the San Francisco 49ers. He was a great competitor. He never complained. Just did his job every Sunday without any fuss, questions or complaints.

One Sunday afternoon in Baltimore I was having breakfast with the crew at the hotel. Nomellini was at the next table with some friends. There had been a little construction work uncompleted in the dining room which was screened off by a heavy wooden screen. As the waitress passed it, her elbow hit the screen and it started to fall right on me. Leo jumped up, grabbed it and saved me an awful whack on the head. I thanked him, not once but a couple of times. I would have had a split head.

That afternoon during the game Nomellini used his hands illegally. I don't ever remember him doing it before. As I was walking the foul and yardage off, he came up to me and still didn't complain about the call. Instead, he said, "I should have let that screen fall on your head this morning in the dining room."

I sensed Leo disapproved of my call.

Perhaps it would have been more comfortable if the screen had fallen on my head. Maybe I wouldn't have felt the cold. It was freezing in Baltimore that Sunday afternoon, and I had forgotten my gloves. When my fingertips get cold, I am cold all over. Leo Nomellini helped me there too.

The San Francisco 49ers had taken the opening kickoff deep in their own end zone. For some unknown reason the receiver started out onto the playing field. He should have taken the touchback. That would have put the ball on his 20-yard line instead of its winding up on his five-yard line. On the first play from scrimmage a 49er halfback fumbled the hand-off from the quarterback. The Colts recovered the ball on the four-yard line. In came the 49ers' defensive team led by Leo Nomellini. He was wearing some nice yellow gloves. The Colts made a couple of yards on their first running play. Apparently, Leo wasn't comfortable with his gloves on. Maybe he couldn't grab the runner like he wanted to. Leo took his nice gloves off, placed them behind the goalpost, and took his position on the defensive line. The Colts went in for a touchdown over the other tackle's spot. Out went the 49ers' defensive team, led by Nomellini, running off the field. I had watched Nomellini take off his gloves and place them behind the goalpost. When Leo ran off, I ran to his gloves, picked them up and put them on quickly. My hands felt warm for the first time that afternoon. Before the next kickoff, Nomellini realized he had left his gloves behind the goalpost. He ran back out onto the field, right to the goalpost, and bent over to pick up his gloves. He then realized that they were gone.

I was willing to help. I was standing under the goalpost, waiting for the TV commercial to end so I could signal for the kickoff to start the action again. I asked Nomellini, "Leo, what are you looking for? Maybe I can help?"

Leo looked up and said, "I left my gloves here. They are gone."

"What did they look like, Leo?"

"Yellow ones. Just like the pair you are wearing." Leo did a double take.

I gave him a knowing look. Before he could say anything, I

said, "Leo, my hands are freezing. You must have left them back on the bench. I'm sure you can find another pair."

Leo grinned at me and said, "Norm, that's two you owe me so far today."

Fred Biletnikoff was one of Oakland's outstanding wide receivers for many years. He was one of the great ends in the business. How he caught the passes he did was beyond me. But he did it constantly. He seemed to come up with the game-winning score every week. It didn't come easy for him, nor does it for any other successful wide receiver. Defensive players grabbed Biletnikoff, held him or chucked him in those first five yards off the scrimmage line whenever they could.

One day Biletnikoff was having his problems. That's par, conversationally speaking, for most great ends. They would like to run out and catch passes without anyone near them. Biletnikoff kept complaining that he was being held and bumped too much. "Hell, Norm, they're almost ripping my shirt off my back."

Finally, Stabler fell back and threw a quick pass to Biletnikoff. I was watching Stabler so no one would rough him. I didn't see what happened downfield. I learned very quickly.

Biletnikoff came running up to me. The shirt was almost off his back, and he was holding part of his jersey in his hand. He screamed, "I told you, I told you. What do you say now?"

I looked at the shirt, looked at him and said, "I say you need a new shirt. What do you think?"

What he thought was different.

Fans always ask me, "Do players yell or talk to one another at the scrimmage line?"

You bet they do. They talk along every scrimmage line throughout the League every Sunday afternoon. The quarterback yells offensive signals, the defensive players yell defensive signals. Some defensive players yell just for the hell of yelling. They are what we referees call yakkers. St. Louis had one of them a few years back. All clubs do. To hear this Cardinal player tell it, "I never foul."

Jim Hart, the quarterback for the Cardinals, dropped back to pass. The offensive guard dropped back to block the pass. He had a unique way of blocking. He held on almost every play. This time his hand strayed too much and he got caught holding the defensive end of Miami. He almost took the defensive end's shirt right off his back. I threw my flag. It was too flagrant, even for me.

As I was walking off the penalty yardage, the guard kept talking to me. "I never held him. Never did."

I kept walking. The guard walked right with me every step. He complained again and again. "I never laid a hand on him. I didn't hold him."

I placed the ball down, turned to the guard and said, "You must have held him. I just measured off fifteen yards for holding."

Somehow, somewhere along the professional football road, fans have received the impression there is a foul on every play of every game. Don't you believe it. The players are pros. Fouls cost yardage. And yards are hard to come by. No player or coach wants to give any of them away.

Sometimes a fan will see a player being held. The howl will go out, "Hey, he's holding, you blind Tom."

The officials see things like that. If the illegal action has no bearing on the play, forget it. The point of attack is what the officials keep in mind. If it's a personal or unnecessary roughness foul, then it's called whether it has anything to do with the play or not. That is also true of pass interference.

A good illustration is a game I refereed in Cleveland. The Cleveland punter kicked the ball a long way, about 60 yards. No one was near the kicker so I looked downfield. The Dallas safety man caught the ball. He started back upfield. I glanced down on the ground as I noticed the Cleveland blocker, and the Dallas man who had been blocked. The Dallas player was on top of the blocker, and using his hands to hold the Cleveland player down. The runner was still 50 yards from the three of us. I stood looking at the two players, especially at the Dallas man holding. I also kept looking downfield to see what was developing. I didn't throw my flag for a holding penalty as both men were just grab-assing and were perfectly happy lying on the ground. Their action had nothing to do with the play. Yet. There was no roughness or personal foul involved. Those fouls are flagged, whether it has anything to do with the play or not.

Then the runner broke free and headed upfield. When he was

about 20 yards from the two players on the ground, I looked at them more closely. The Dallas player still held the Cleveland man and used his hands to keep him down. The same situation as a couple of seconds ago. But then I threw my penalty flag. The scene had changed dramatically. The man being held now had an opportunity to make the play. And was trying to get up. That was a foul for illegal holding. The very same holding that I had allowed to go unpenalized had become a foul. The Dallas player was gaining an unfair advantage. That's why I was there.

There are no assassins on the field during a professional football game. It makes for good copy when a player says, "I play tough. I play for keeps. I'm the intimidator. I want them to know that I'm coming at them."

Who is he scaring? No one. The other players are as big and tough and as aggressive. If anyone backs up to talk like that, he backs right out of the League. Occasionally a player becomes overly aggressive. Most experienced players have their eyes open at all times. They want to see who is coming at them and from where. It's when they relax away from the play that someone might legally block or bang them from the side. Instinctively, they scream, "Foul, foul."

These players are big men, strong men, fast men. Any legal collision is bound to smart a bit. An illegal collision hurts that much more, for the player fouled doesn't expect it. Over the years I have seen many, many more serious injuries on legal plays than on illegal hits.

Years ago, before the exhaustive coverage by television and the excellent NFL films, a player could get away with some illegal action. Not anymore. Even if the game officials miss a serious illegal hit on a player, the League in reviewing every game film will pick it up. The Commissioner will then take whatever action he believes the situation requires. It would be better to see the foul when it happens, but officials do the best they can.

I have cringed and winced many times when I see how an O. J. Simpson, an Earl Campbell, a Walter Payton or any other running back gets tackled. Legal all the way, but I don't know how they ever get up. But they do. And go through the same thing many times and very well. They do take a pounding, but it's all by the rules.

In all the years I've refereed in professional football, I can't honestly remember more than a few isolated incidents of deliberate injuring of an opponent. And I like to think my flag flew, and that player left for the day.

Fights occur on the field. I'm surprised they don't happen more often. It's a collision sport which brings out bitter hurts. But the players are real pros and so are the officials. Fights occur in high school and college games. They occur on the school grounds and even at home.

Professional football is a highly emotional game, and people get excited. It's all in a day's work. It's nothing personal. The real pros leave their feelings on the field each Sunday. Too much happens every week. Players, coaches and referees have to move on to the next game. When Bert Bell hired me years ago, the only advice he gave me was "Norm, professional football is a tough, hard-hitting emotional game. Everybody out on the field gets excited. And mad. Just remember why you are out there. You can't and are not to get emotional, excited or mad at anyone. Just provide the emotional stability. And keep the peace."

Years ago, former Supreme Court Justice Harold Burton in a television interview reached into sport for a metaphor to explain the function of the Supreme Court: "It isn't that referees are infallible or perfect, but if there is going to be any contest—a long contest, a close contest, a hard contest—and you're not going to break up into a riot or a squabble, you'd better agree on a referee before you start. Take his decision and go ahead with the game. And in government it's the same principle."

Color Me Black
and White with Stripes

Even though too many fans seem to believe referees can't do anything right, they also seem to think the job is a day at the beach. They say, "You referees are really lucky. You have the best seat in the house, get in free, and get to watch the game up real close. It sure looks like a fun afternoon. Easy too."

I am often asked, "How do you get a job like that? I've thought I would like to spend a couple of hours like that."

Horseshit!

Why would anyone think the referees have it easy? Why would they assume no preparation is needed, and nothing is required in the way of dedication? Yet that's what I hear all the time. That's the attitude of people who know little about our business. There's no guesswork out on the field. The job requires a whole lot more than having free Sunday afternoons.

Let me repeat that. There is no guesswork in our business. When I think of guesswork, I think of Lem Barney, the tough cornerback of the Detroit Lions. He never had a bad day when I refereed. That's because he seldom had a bad day. Barney was a con artist in his own way. He never missed an opportunity to speak kindly to the referee. Whenever I went out on the field to start the game, it was always "Hey, Doc, how are you? How's things in Los Angeles? When I quit playing, I'm going to be a referee. Got any good tips for me to remember? I sure would like to be as good as you." I smiled, for I had been that route many times. They are all pros, players and con artists.

Barney was called for defensive pass interference in the second quarter. I gave the signal. Television needed a time-out, so I took it after I had measured off the penalty. Barney was still fuming. He put on a great show of indignation. He got the home crowd on my back with his act. I told him to knock it off.

"Okay, okay. I guess you don't want me to needle you, do you?"

"Lem," I answered, "if I could guess as good as that, I could work an extra ten years and never make a mistake."

Let's get to what coaches and players say. Surprisingly, not too much. And seldom in language that you don't use at home. Never any of the words that you hear in movies or read in books. No referee worth his salt would take it. Neither would the League office permit it. Most of it, though serious, is part of an act. It's an honest routine that has to be acted out. If the referee's call is close and affects the outcome of a ball game—hell, what else can a coach do but scream? Who is there to scream at? He can't castigate the owner, he can't ridicule his players, and he can't blame the press. Who's left? You guessed it. The referee is the only game in town after a tough loss. Sometimes even the most even-tempered coaches get upset. One winning coach in the midwest, a most successful one, really let a referee know how he felt. And that was before the game even started. The Marine Corps color guard came out onto the field to post the colors. The band struck up the national anthem. The coach took off his hat. The referee, who was walking up and down the sideline prior to kickoff, was walking past the coach when the anthem started. The referee took off his cap and placed it over his heart. Not quite. He didn't get the hat all the way up to his heart when the coach looked at the referee next to him and said, "Would you mind standing someplace else when they play 'The Star-Spangled Banner'? I don't want you too close to me."

When I started refereeing in the professional football league, whenever I heard a coach call me a name I hadn't been called before, I listed it in my book of most forgettable names. I still have the book. But there aren't too many names listed. Especially for the last 15 years. Over the years the coaches and players paid for their privilege of free speech. Usually 15 yards' worth. That's what I charged them. My first year or so I was a blind sonavabitch, a no-good bastard, a horseshit referee and mole-eyed. Mole-eyed? After several 15-yard walk-offs, the word spread. I still might have been a blind sonavabitch, a no-good bastard and a horseshit referee, but no one ever mentioned it anymore. At least not aloud. If they did, my flag would fly. Fast. I told them, "If you want to say something, say it. But be certain I can't hear it. If I do, it's fifteen for sure."

I particularly remember a coach in New York. And what he told me. It was the first time I had heard what he yelled at me. The Giants had used up their third time-out, so that meant a visit to the coach. I personally had to tell him that his team didn't have any more time-outs left. Each team is allowed three time-outs per half. For some reason the coach was upset. Maybe it was the holding penalty I had just called which brought the ball back after a 40-yard run. It doesn't matter why he was upset, but he was. I walked over to him as he was grimacing, waving his arms and sputtering. He must have been sputtering, for he was too much of a pro to spit at me.

"Coach," I said, "that's your last time-out this half."

He continued to wave his hands. Close. Too close. He shouted, "Norm, you're an astigmatic one-eyed referee."

I was shocked. Shocked because it was a new word to me at the time. I thought it was a dirty word. That cost him 15 yards.

I got more help from Van Brocklin when he was coaching in the League than I did from the rule book. Whether I needed it or not didn't make any difference. I got it anyway. I even got his help when he was a star quarterback. He kept the officials on their toes. I liked him.

It happened the first year Van Brocklin was coaching Minnesota. I had to call a clip near the Minnesota Vikings' bench. It was close. I was walking off the yardage when I heard The Dutchman's voice ring out loud and clear. "Norm, give it a look. It wasn't a clip. Open your eyes."

I never answer a coach's scream from the sideline. I always ignore the bleeding. But this time I didn't ignore it. I answered Van Brocklin, "Coach, I call them like I see them."

Van Brocklin didn't hesitate. He came right back with "I know that. But I would rather you call them like they happen, not like you see them."

One day in Detroit Alex Karras got a free one from me. People forget what a first-rate player Alex Karras was. Howard Cosell and Frank Gifford used to kid him on the Monday night football game. But don't ever forget that Karras was a great defensive tackle. He has now blossomed out into quite an ad-libber and actor. A good one too.

For years I didn't know Karras knew how to talk. He never said a word on the field to the referee. He just played hard, tough and clean football. Except for one time. It was a cold, drizzly day in Detroit. I threw my flag on Karras for tripping a runner who had blown by him. Karras thought he hadn't tripped the runner. Anyway, the runner went down and so did my penalty flag. Alex Karras reacted, and that's a mild way of putting it. He spoke, which surprised me. Oh, how he spoke.

It finally got to the point of almost no return. "Alex," I said, "enough is enough. You've had your say. Now say no more."

Karras saw that I was put out. He smiled (I think it was a smile) and said, "Ref, can I be penalized for thinking?"

"No way, Alex. No penalty for thinking." I was grinning.

Karras stared at me. "Well, I think you're a blind sonavabitch."

Chalk one up for the defensive tackle. He got his ad-lib training on me.

Coaches might have called me a lot over the years—most of it under their breath—but never have they ever called me dishonest or crooked. Not even once. And that applies to all the other National Football League officials.

Isn't it interesting? Amazing is a better word for it. From what we read in the papers, hundreds and hundreds of millions of dollars are bet every Sunday on professional football games. Not once has there been any hint of a referee being part of the action. Doesn't that tell you something about the caliber of the referees in the NFL? Since professional football started, in the early twenties, there has never been any suspicion directed toward a referee's call. It's open season on a referee's judgment, but never on his integrity. That's because NFL officials are successful men in their regular vocations, and they have developed standards and attitudes that are foreign to anything illegal. These men do not need the money refereeing. Don't get me wrong, however. They never can pay enough for the work a referee does on the field. Just try

having a football game on the honor system. Let players admit a
foul. Or call one on themselves. Picture, if you can, a long touchdown run. Fans are screaming. It was the winning touchdown.
Wait a minute. The right tackle comes up to the referee and says,
"Ref, I held on that last play. It is no touchdown. I'm sorry. But I
cheated. And I am ashamed of myself."

Don't hold your breath. It will never happen. For several reasons. The big one is that players don't honestly know when they
foul. And—players don't realize that they foul. At least that's
what they tell me. All the time. I hope they believe what they say.
Even so, I have a strong feeling that the guys in the striped shirts
will always be a part of the game.

In the development of the NFL since 1922 to its present popular acceptance, the players, the coaches and the sports writers
have all become more knowledgeable. Perhaps the greatest development of all has been the consistent integrity and dedication of
the officials. From a purely biased viewpoint, I believe that
officials have come along the furthest in the past 25 years. I'm certain some will say they had to. And others will say, "You've come
a long way, baby—but not far enough."

I hit the lecture tour often. I travel all over and speak to different groups. I particularly remember one night I spoke for a medi-
cal group. Doctors, radiologists, anesthesiologists—the whole
bunch. I charged them a good fee, which surprised them. I didn't
want them to think that they were the only people who charged a
lot. I shudder when I think of my introduction. If Commissioner
Rozelle had been in the audience that night, my career as a referee would have been over. I was the featured speaker at their
lavish dinner. That particular week the newspapers all over the
country had been running special features on gambling on professional sports. No definite accusations, but much speculative
writing.

It was a huge affair and a large crowd. The master of ceremonies wanted everyone to know that their organization had gone to
great expense to get me to speak that night. He introduced me in
two sentences. "Ladies and gentlemen, I would like to present our
guest speaker for tonight. He's the best referee that money
can buy."

Lots of luck and a good bounce of the ball keep a referee working. It's better to be lucky than good. At least it seems that way. After a few years in the League with national television exposure, any referee gets on the banquet circuit. Some speeches are freebies. No charge. Especially for a charitable group.

The Southern California Football Hall of Fame Foundation had me as a speaker. The master of ceremonies was John McKinley, owner of one of the largest mortuaries in southern California. He introduced me and said, "Norm knows we don't have a budget for speakers. We can't even give him a letter opener or a plaque. However, I want him to know that I am offering him a ten percent discount on any funeral this month. Nontransferable, of course."

It got a laugh. Like whenever I was knocked down on the field. From the back of the room a voice yelled, "And I'll be glad to pay the other ninety percent. I've seen him referee."

That got a bigger laugh.

The Culver City Monday Morning Quarterback Club had a unique moneymaking gimmick. After I had finished speaking, I was asked to mention any type of foul. Someone in the audience would be called upon by the president to give the signal for that foul. A miss meant anything from a one- to ten-dollar fine.

I went through the signals, starting with "offsides" and gradually worked my way up to the tougher signals. Some fouls seldom happen, and unless you're an official, you have no reason to know the signal.

My last one was "Here's a tough one for the next guy. One player punches another player and knocks him down. The referee throws him out of the game for unsportsmanlike conduct. What is the signal for unsportsmanlike conduct?"

The president of the club called upon the chief of police, a most active member. The chief got up, thought a minute, then stroked his right index finger on his left index finger. Sort of a "Shame, shame on you" sign that kids do when someone is naughty.

It cost him ten bucks. I liked his signal though. It would have made a hit on national TV, but not in the League office.

Do you remember when I said that a referee has to be perfect the first game of the season? And then get better every week that follows? As a referee, he has to prove himself again and again every week. He's tested every Sunday afternoon. Millions grade him. Not just the League office. How would you like to have an instant replay camera on your back all day long, checking every move you make? In our line of work even our best friends will tell us.

Think of how many patients die on the operating table. Still, people remember all the successful operations a doctor has done. A quarterback can muff a play, but be forgiven because he also makes great plays. A coach can be forgiven for losing a big game because the fans remember big games he has won. But a referee is only as good as his last call. He'd better pray it was the right one.

There is a popular belief that only two teams are involved in a professional football game. Don't you believe it. The next time you watch a game, look the field over carefully. You will see a third team—seven fellows in striped shirts and white pants, each with a whistle in his mouth.

But we—the third team—don't mind passing unnoticed. We live by the rule "If they don't know who's working the ball game, you've had a great day." The degree of anonymity an official achieves with the coaches, players, and spectators is quite often the degree of his success. Of course, no official can go unnoticed forever. Sooner or later, he will be booed by the crowd. And worse yet, some people will learn his name. A football official lives by that one word and that one word alone: anonymity. If they don't know who's working, you can't get into trouble.

Art McNally, Supervisor of Officials in the National Football League, introduced a new official at our annual football clinic a few years ago. "Fellows, I want you to meet Jim Poole. He's a new back judge in the League. He comes highly recommended. We've watched him work and he's a good one."

The other officials gave him a courtesy round of applause. McNally waited until the applause had died down, turned to Poole and said, "That's the last time you'll ever hear applause as an official in the NFL."

Smart man, that McNally. He's been there, walked those white lines with his striped shirt on his back. And heard it all.

I remember a new official who wasn't new for long. In fact, he wasn't around for long. Just one season. That was one season too much. One day in New Orleans we had a tight call on the sideline. The line judge, the new man, was right on the play. It was a short forward pass close to the sideline. The new man's position on the play was great. His call was the problem. He had called it an incomplete pass. He thought the receiver's second step had just touched the sideline. The New Orleans coach was all over him. It happened right in front of his bench. I really felt for the new man. I ran over to quiet the coach down. Just as I reached the two of them, I heard the line judge tell the coach, "Yah, it was a close play. I could have called it either way. I chose to call it out of bounds."

The coach was furious. That triggered him even more. I remember the coach's answer. It was a good one. "You don't have a choice. It's either good or bad."

The coach was right. I don't mean on that call. An official doesn't have a choice. No matter how close or tight it is. It is either good or bad. A foul or not a foul. Close only counts in horseshoes or parachute jumping.

After a tough ball game in Baltimore not too long ago, I was hustling to catch my plane. I left the dressing room carrying my traveling bag and really moved out. As I was walking through the crowd, two youngsters about ten years old stopped me.

The smaller kid asked, "Hey, how about your autograph?"

"Not now, son, not now. I'm in a rush to catch a plane."

"Please, Mister."

"Okay. Let me have your pencil. I'm really in a rush."

I signed my name "Norm Schachter, #56." I handed the signed paper and pencil back to the smaller kid.

The youngster took the paper, looked at my name and asked, "Who are you?"

Before I could answer, the other kid said, "If he has to tell you who he is, he ain't."

I guess he was right. The smaller kid threw the paper away.

Unlike baseball umpiring, pro football officiating is an avocation, not a vocation. It is not a full-time job. We work on a yearly contract. If you make too many judgment errors, you're gone. We get paid by the game. Salaries vary with experience. Referees with 10 years experience get $800 per regular season game. We do have a pension plan. Post-season games pay extra and the Super Bowl fee is now $3,000 a man. Per diem and first-class travel are on the League. It is a first-class operation and they expect us to be first class. Though there is just one game on Sunday afternoon that an official works, most officials after a tough ball game feel as if they have worked a full week. And in a sense they have. It isn't just one afternoon's work load. Most officials review rules and play situations throughout the week. That's a lot of reviewing and that's every day of every week for the entire season. Since there are now four pre-season games and sixteen regular games, that's a total of twenty weeks without counting the play-off games.

Each week each official is given a three-part weekly review quiz. It consists of a true-false page of general questions on rules. It also consists of a definite rule which is broken down into ten questions. And finally, the last part of the weekly review quiz is on troublesome plays with spot of enforcement. That's the spot from which the referee starts walking off the yardage for the foul. None of the questions is theoretical in nature; they are based on plays that have occurred throughout the years. This weekly review quiz is the basis of the crew conference on Saturday night.

The third team, the officials, work as a seven-man crew. The same crew members work together all season, and generally, unless someone gets fired or retires, season after season. Crew members and game assignments are received from the National Football League, our boss. Most people don't seem to realize that we work for the League, not for the individual clubs. I'm sure that many coaches and owners would like to carry their own crew of officials. But we're paid by the League and the League only. We have nothing to do with the clubs, except to work their games as representatives of the League office. Officials are very careful not to be overly familiar with owners, coaches or players. The League frowns on any official offering congratulations on a win, and does not want us to go into either team's dressing room except on official business. It doesn't say anything about a doctor's visit there.

One game Cleveland had with the New York Giants sticks in my mind. I can't forget it. I carry a reminder (a scar) on my left leg. Every time I spot that scar on my leg, I think back to that particular day in Cleveland.

Remember Jim Brown? The same one who is a movie star now. He was one of the all-time greats. Best fullback I ever worked. Maybe O. J. Simpson can take a place alongside of him. Jim

Brown was great. They had to surround him to stop him. This particular day Jim Brown had a helluva day against the New York Giants. But he always had a helluva day against everyone.

Jim Brown's runs that day aren't what stay with me. My left shinbone reminds me of him. He had just made a tough first down. I reached in too fast to get the ball. And his leg whipped around. His cleats caught my left shinbone and ripped the leg open. It really smarted. It wasn't the time to call an injury time-out. Not for the referee anyway. Cleveland was on the move. And I wasn't about to stop their drive. The Giants couldn't, so why should I? The Browns went in to score soon after.

After the game I rushed to the dressing room to take a look at my left skinbone. I couldn't get the stocking off the shinbone. The blood had coagulated and the stocking was stuck to my leg. Finally, I worked it tenderly and got it loose. I realized I had to have a team doctor look at it. I started into the Giants' dressing room. I suddenly thought that I had better check. I saw Sam Huff. "Hey, Sam, who won today?"

Huff looked at me. He thought I was a wise-ass. "You and I both lost."

I hadn't really known. I walked down to the Cleveland dressing room. I had their team doctor look at it. I wasn't about to walk into a loser's dressing room. Not to get help.

We make our own plane reservations. I average over 125,000 miles per season. When they say I am high, that's what they mean. I have been lucky in that I have never missed a ball game. Only came close one time. I remember leaving my home in Los Angeles one Saturday morning for a game in Pittsburgh. We flew into some rough weather and had to land in Kansas City. I took the only flight that night to Chicago and stayed there until Sunday morning. At 6:00 A.M. I was at last able to get on a plane to Pittsburgh. We landed there at noon. I got to the stadium at 12:30 P.M. and gave the signal to start the game at 1:05 P.M. Fortunately for me, it turned out to be an easy game with few fouls.

All seven members of our third team are good friends with one another. We have to be. After a tough ball game and a hassle or two, no one is going to step forward and say "Friend" to me. I always remember that the only friends I have during a football game are the other six officials. And then I keep an eye on them.

The crew members arrive at different times on Saturday. The first man to arrive in the city that day (and it's usually Jack Fette, the line judge) rents a car and tries to meet the others. We've told Fette that if he loses his driving license, we'll get another line judge. If possible, the fellows wait for one another at the airport and come in as a group.

The League office makes hotel reservations for all the crews throughout the season. Before the start of the season, the officials select the hotels they prefer for each League city. The very best hotels are selected. It's first cabin all the way. We'll need our rest, especially if we have to make a run for it after the game.

Though all seven of us live in different sections of the country, we always manage to meet at the hotel around 5:00 P.M. for our first meeting. That's really kickoff time for our team. There we review our last game. Every possible foul, no-foul, and controversial call is rehashed. Everyone goes over what we heard, saw and read about our last game. When we've exhausted that topic, we review the calls we've heard or read about from the other games. With their inquiries about unusual calls from the previous Sunday, football fans keep the phones at the League office ringing all week long.

Besides the weekly review quizzes we go over, Saturday afternoon is also "book time." Every week one fellow is assigned a rule to discuss in depth at our Saturday meeting. One week the field judge may go over all possible pass interference calls, trap plays, and pick-off plays. He questions us on penalties, rules interpretations and the tough-call areas of pass interference. When he is through, another crew member is assigned a rule for the following week. It might, for example, be the umpire who will discuss holding and illegal use of the hands. Everyone will get his chance to shine and be head man on a different Saturday. Our rule book may not be too racy, but we spend more time reading it than we do *Playboy* magazine.

That takes us up to seven to seven-thirty. Then it's time to eat. Meals too are a together thing. And we never take a drink at dinner. Liquor or wine is definitely out. Coffee and tea are par for the course. That makes sense. Can you imagine what a fan would think if he saw the football officials having a social drink with their Saturday night meal? Especially if the team he bet on loses and one of the officials he saw at dinner has made the big call. No matter how right the call would be, you can bet that that man would say, "What the hell can you expect? I saw that guy drinking last night at dinner and he acted drunk to me even then." As a result the League has a rigid rule that no one, and I mean no one, can take a drink from the time he leaves his house on Saturday morning until after the game on Sunday afternoon. It's a great rule for it protects us from all possible misunderstanding.

I remember speaking at a golf club sports banquet one night after the season had ended. My host that night was a nice guy. He met me, took me into the recreation room and bar and said, "What are you drinking?"

"Thanks, Ed. Nothing right now. I never drink before I give a speech."

"Only before a game, huh?" Everyone is a comedian.

How wrong he was. If any official takes a drink from the time he leaves home until after the game, he's gone. Fired. Right now. Best rule they have.

We never discuss football at dinner, for one of us might say something jokingly and be overheard and misunderstood. Politics and other sports are taken care of at this time, and for guys who hate to be second-guessed, we certainly do our share of it. Maybe second-guessing is a part of human nature. Gerry Hart once told me after a tough call and lots of booing, "People who think the President has a tough job should be an official in the NFL."

After dinner it's back to work for "Saturday Night at the Movies." It isn't cartoon time, either. We watch the film of our last game. Throughout it everybody comments freely. It's "Back it up, let's look at that foul again. There? What do you think?" and "Good thing I didn't call that a clip. Damn good block. Right? Real close." This goes on for two to three hours. How long depends upon how difficult a game it was the previous week.

When I check into the hotel on Saturday, the bell captain has a film projector ready for me. The home team has sent it over for our use; the line judge will return it to them the next day at the stadium. On Tuesday or Wednesday the League office air-freighted the previous game film and that is waiting at the hotel for me. Our umpire will return it to the League office on the following Monday. Ships it back. Unless one of our crew members wants to review further at home during the week.

There are five reels in our game film. One is for kicks: kickoffs, field goals, punts and try-for-points. Two are on the offensive plays, one reel for each half. The remaining two reels are defensive ones, again, one for each half.

With each film package we get a play-by-play résumé of the game. It's the same résumé reporters receive in the press box. It details every play, the yardage to be made, the spot of the snap and the position of the ball on the field. It includes every foul called with the player's number. Written on the résumé are comments from the League supervisors who have reviewed the film and made notations on the sheets. Things like "Look at offensive #76. Is he using his hands illegally?" or "If you had to call this play again, would you call it a clip?" It keeps us on our toes. Our game performance is graded by the supervisors from the films and that determines the play-off assignments. They have everything you do in black and white. No secrets from them. Before the filming of the games in such detail, we referees could say, "We were blocked out on that play" or "The man never was touched." Not anymore though.

We also go over everything I heard on Monday from the Supervisor of Officials, Art McNally, when I phoned in my report of the game. The League had already heard from the game observer, newspaper reporters and the coaches. These comments are relayed to me, and I relay them to the crew along with the League's comments on the game film. As we review the film, we try not to second-guess ourselves. Enough people do that for us. We use the film as a teaching device and a learning guide. We're constantly trying to improve our mechanics and position on the field. We stop the film, rerun it and dissect it thoroughly. When we are finished with it, we review what we're going to concentrate on the next day. By this time it is around 11 o'clock, and we are ready to call it a night.

We meet again for breakfast at nine. Once again, we try not to discuss football, but occasionally people recognize us anyway. We are especially careful not to get into any conversation with strangers, nor do we allow them to sit at our table. You never know for sure who some people are. It is so easy for gossip to start.

We arrive at the stadium two hours before kickoff. Our contract requires us to be in our dressing room at this time for our pregame conference. No one is exempt from this pre-game conference. If someone isn't there, he had better damn well have a good excuse.

Everyone gets into the act. Hometown fans are frustrated co-medians when it comes to referees. We were early one Sunday afternoon in New Orleans as we wanted to be sure to have enough time to find our dressing room and have our pre-game conference. It was the first time I had gone into the Superdome. The Superdome is a great place to work a ball game. But it was new to me, and on the way to the dressing room I took a turn and started to walk toward the left. I told the crew, "Follow me, it's this way."

A policeman on duty saw me and yelled, "Hey, Ref, where are you going?"

"Dressing room. Got to get ready for the game," I yelled back.

The cop grunted, "It's the other way. Hell, you haven't started the game yet, and you have already made one wrong call."

One wrong call a day wouldn't be too bad. Especially before the game.

In our dressing room before a game, as referee I conduct the pre-game conference. Its primary purpose is to review basic principles of officiating as they relate to the particular game. There isn't time for a complete review of the rules, and one wouldn't make sense anyway. All the crew members know the rules and their interpretations. A knowledge of teams' systems and individual player habits is valuable in the pre-game conference. This time is more profitably spent in going over items that might create problems on the field.

It was a good thing we did that one time at a ball park. Especially so as it was one of the early games in the season. It was a bang-bang catch near the corner of the field on the sideline and end line. Both the back judge and field judge were right on the play. That was a problem though. The field judge gave the signal for a touchdown and the back judge gave the signal for an incomplete pass and no touchdown. He had seen the second step of the receiver touch the sideline. I ran down to discuss the situation.

Before I could say anything, the field judge came right up and said, "I went too fast. No touchdown. I didn't get a good look at that second step. I should have looked at the back judge. It was his call. Forget that I signaled. No score. Forget it."

I was willing to forget and forgive. But not the coach. It didn't matter, for we went with the back judge's call. It was his call, and he was right on the play.

That is stuff we review in our pre-game conference. Every

week. We look for help if we don't get a good shot at the play. It takes guts for a man to back down. And it takes guts to work in this League.

I remember another game where I was personally involved. Fortunately, it was just a mixed-up signal. The Rams had fumbled the ball around their 10-yard line. There was a scramble for the ball. Players piled on one another. The ball was somewhere underneath the pileup. I had had a good look at it before the pileup. I had seen the Ram player fall on the ball and lie on it. I signaled Rams' ball and pointed in the direction they were going. Unfortunately, the umpire also signaled. But he signaled the other way. However, he had yelled, "Rams' ball" when he had blown his whistle. He had just signaled the wrong way. He was completely turned around, but he had the right call. There we were. The two of us. Both staring right into each other's face. Not more than a yard apart. He pointing one way and me pointing the other way. Someone snapped that picture. I had a copy of it, but I got rid of it the same day. It didn't matter, for I got lots of them in the mail. That's one picture I could do without. It was a good thing that the umpire had yelled, "Rams' ball." Otherwise we would have had a hard time selling the call. That's part of our job. Salesmanship. I found out early in my career that you can only sell a call when you are right.

Let's stay with that fumbled-ball situation for a second. If we had had a difference of opinion, I, as referee and the man in charge of the crew, could not have overruled the other official's judgment call. It is then we would have had a crew conference to find out what the other officials had seen. A majority vote decides, especially when both officials on the play claim that they were 1,000 percent correct. And not a doubt in their minds. It pays not to signal too quickly, especially if the ball is loose. Or dead.

When we go out on the field 30 minutes before kickoff, we're ready. During this half hour all seven officials have definite responsibilities which have to be performed. The referee checks with the coaches to see if there will be any unusual plays that might surprise the officials. The umpire checks all players whose hands are bandaged or taped as well as all players wearing special protective equipment; he has to be certain that they will not injure other players. The head linesman locates the yardage chains, checks them out and reviews procedures with the chain crew. The chain crew (boxman, two rodmen and alternate) are not part of the officiating crew. They are appointed by the Commissioner from each League city. They are local men.

The line judge contacts each coach and informs him of the official time, schedule of kickoff and any pre-toss program. He also locates the field telephone operator and announcer. The line judge really tells the coaches the official time in the dressing rooms an hour before kickoff. The official time is obtained from the television truck outside the stadium.

The back judge and the side judge check the field and the markings. They usually start on the 50-yard line on opposite sides of the field and go to their left around the boundary lines.

Three minutes before the kickoff, the referee meets with the two team captains in the center of the field for the coin toss. He signals which team will receive and which team will kick off. We're now ready for the game. And away we go.

Perhaps a word or two on what the officials do before, during and after a play will give a better understanding of our job. Let me draw a diagram for you. Look at the diagram and locate the seven officials. Every official has a definite area of responsibility. We just don't run all over the field and look for fouls. Many times I have no idea what is happening at some distance away from me on the field. I have my own territory to patrol and that's what I am paid for. And responsible for. A referee can get into trouble very easily when he lets his eyes and mind wander over to another area. That is the crew concept.

Here's a pro set formation from the line of scrimmage. It shows clearly where all the seven officials originally stand before the play action gets under way. When any play starts from scrimmage (with the center snap), these are the spots the seven men take. Take a look at the picture on the next page.

The referee (R) has general oversight and control of the game. He is the final authority for the score. He stands behind the offensive team, 8 to 12 yards to the right of the quarterback. When I had my Achilles injury, I usually stayed 14 or 15 yards deep. I wasn't about to get knocked down. My field judge, George Ellis, also had an injury and played his position downfield a little deeper than he should have. About 30 to 35 yards deep away from

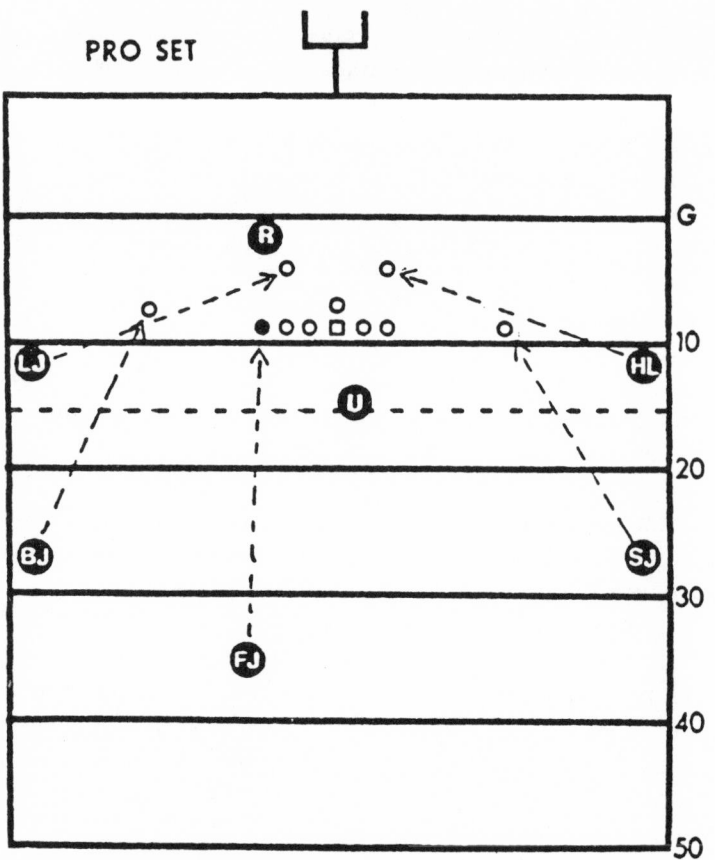

PRO SET

the scrimmage line. Ellis told me, "Between the two of us, we have the whole length of the field covered. No one could get by either one of us."

The referee (R) stays on the right (unless there is a left-handed quarterback like Zorn of Seattle or Stabler of Houston), for one of the toughest calls is whether the pass is started or not. The referee must assume a position that affords a clear view of all backfield players. He is the one you see go out and give the signals for television and he enforces all penalties. He keeps the spectators informed through the small microphone he has taped to his chest. He had better know when the switch is on, for a lot of things out on the field are better left unsaid.

The umpire (U) plays directly behind the defense, about three to five yards back of the ball. He watches the interior line play.

He learns very quickly to move, for the smart quarterbacks will use him as a post or screen for forward passes. When an official gets hit, nine out of ten times he is the umpire. And nine out of ten times that will get the biggest cheer of the afternoon. When Dave Hamilton, a good umpire, first came into the League, he worked his first pro game with me. He was knocked down on three of the first five plays. He was too eager to show his moves. I finally had to go up to him and say, "Dave, I don't know whether the League office mentioned it to you or not. But you are not supposed to tackle or block as an official. You had better get your ass back about seven yards until you get the feel of the position or you won't live to work a second game in this league." He moved back. He's still working. Good too.

The head linesman (HL) takes a position at the end of the line. Not too close to the end because the play will sweep by him. He handles the chain crew and all plays in his side zone—offsides, illegal motion and holding of the end and flanker.

The line judge (LJ) stands across from the head linesman; he has very basic responsibilities. He checks to see whether a pass thrown behind the line is a forward or backward one, whether a scrambling quarterback throws a pass behind or beyond the line of scrimmage, and whether there is illegal motion on line and shift plays.

The back judge (BJ) and the side judge (SJ) are responsible for picking up the runner in their side zone when the runner crosses the line of scrimmage. Both of them spot the ball on runs that develop away from them. Pass interference is also one of their big calls. They play from 15 to 18 yards off the ball downfield from the head linesman and line judge, depending upon the side of the field they are on. An important call is "chucking," which is illegal use of hands on an eligible receiver after five yards downfield.

The field judge (FJ) is the deep man. Almost in the middle of the field. He keeps busy. You may think he is a spectator or selling programs, but he's moving and thinking all 60 minutes of a ball game. He stands about 20 to 25 yards downfield. He watches for pass interference, holding of the tight end, first touching of a kick and out-of-bounds plays. He is especially careful not to let the ball get between him and the goal line or end line. He checks the

30-second count. That's how much time a team is allowed to get the ball in play after the referee gives his signal to play. That's the chopping sign of the hand that you see a referee give on every play that starts.

Though the referee is in charge of the game and crew, he cannot overrule an official's judgment call. All seven officials have equal responsibility. A rule interpretation can be discussed, but never a judgment call unless the official has been blocked out and must look for help. It's when we don't look for help at times that we get into difficulty.

A knowledge of the rules is very important. Judgment and common sense are even more important. Some NFL officials are more knowledgeable than others on rules, but all of them have tremendous judgment. That's what they're paid for.

Before every game I tell the crew, "Keep your eye on the ball. Don't blow your whistle unless you see the ball." I learned the hard way. I still wake up nights thinking how I almost blew a call. And my job.

It was in Washington. The Redskins had a third-and-inches play on their own 34-yard line. If ever there was a time to pick up the first down on a plunge, this was it. It started that way too. The quarterback—I think it was Norm Snead—handed off to the fullback, who dived over the center for an apparent first down. I moved in quickly, too quickly. It was a fake hand-off and a dandy. I was about to blow my whistle to kill the play when I heard this tremendous roar from the crowd. I looked up to see Bobby Mitchell alone in the end zone, waiting for the long forward pass to reach him. I didn't blow the whistle, for I literally froze. I didn't blow the play. But it was real close. Now I don't care how long it takes me to find the ball. I don't blow the whistle unless I see the ball.

If an official blows his whistle when he shouldn't have, like not seeing the ball, that's called an inadvertent whistle. That's the name for it in the rule book. That isn't the expression officials hear though. The inadvertent whistle is one you blow at the wrong time. It's a tough call to swallow. The whistle kills everything— the play, the action and the referee all in one blow.

Eddie LeBaron could do everything with the ball except eat it.

Small as he is, he was amazing when he played. When he started to hand off the ball, his opponents never were sure whether he kept it or dished it off. Neither was I. He was a magician with the ball after he took the center snap. Especially one afternoon in Yankee Stadium against the Giants the first year Dallas was in the League. I had known LeBaron when he was with the Washington Redskins and also from his college days at the University of the Pacific in Stockton, California. I always had to concentrate extra hard the afternoons LeBaron quarterbacked.

Before that game in Yankee Stadium, LeBaron spoke to me right before the coin toss at the start of the game. "The referee was fooled on a hand-off last week and blew his whistle inadvertently. It really hurt us. Stay on your toes today, Norm."

It was a high-scoring, exciting game. I watched LeBaron like a hawk. The ball was in my sight whenever he took the snap. I got careless one time. LeBaron took the snap, handed off to his tailback, who ran wide. I was right with the runner when he was tackled. And blew him dead with a loud whistle. There was this little problem though. LeBaron never gave up the ball on the hand-off to his runner. He kept the damn thing. He had been spotted by a defensive player who also had kept his eyes on LeBaron all the time. Eddie was tackled after a short gain. It was right after I had already blown my whistle. I was just lucky. He could have run or thrown a pass for a touchdown which wouldn't have counted, for I had already blown my whistle to kill the play. That's why I always say that it's better to be lucky than good.

As LeBaron was returning to his huddle, he reminded me of our pre-game discussion. Before he could say too much, I told him, "Eddie, you're perfect. You're batting a thousand the last two weeks. Fooled a referee last week. And one this week. Too bad the guy who tackled you wasn't a referee instead of a player. You would have gotten all three."

We officials receive constant bulletins throughout the year. The League office alerts us to any new wrinkles or problems that have developed. During the summer, the officials meet for a four-day clinic in which they review movies of calls of previous years, the mechanics of each position and positioning. They especially go over techniques. All possible types of offenses and defenses are re-

viewed for officiating positioning. Unusual situations from previous seasons are discussed thoroughly. It is not a second-guessing
game. If there were mistakes made, they won't be made a second
time. There is also a review of the rules test. The League mails a
rules-review examination of 200 questions. The questions, incorpo-
rate the various rules within play situations. It is an open-book
exam; the officials have two months to complete the test and return it. Most officials who live within a reasonable distance of
each other get together from five to seven times over a period of
six weeks to discuss the test questions. Our group on the West
Coast—not to be confused with our crew—meets one afternoon a
week in April and May from 4:00 P.M. until nine that evening;
then we all go out to dinner and talk football. It is a complete
rules review. I know, for I make up the test questions. That's one
sure way to have the answers. Always thinking.

By now I'm sure you understand why an official really hurts
when someone believes he just drops by on a Sunday afternoon to
work a couple of hours. It's not a couple of hours. It's years of experience, hours every week of reviewing the rule book and thinking football. And it's a complete dedication to a job that makes
sense and is enjoyable. It's like my Marine Corps experience. I
wouldn't take a million dollars to do it again, but I wouldn't have
missed it for the world.

Besides his uniform, there are two things a pro official needs to
have. One is a basic understanding of the rule book. The other is a
thorough knowledge of the *Officials' Manual*. But neither book
will teach how to make instant decisions, adjust to emergencies,
show poise and temper control, be courteous and considerate yet
firm and decisive and be consistent in your calls. Proper preparation can eliminate potential problems. Competency and integrity
are basic requirements. You can't learn those qualities from
any book.

I well remember a Green Bay–Dallas game one day in Dallas.
Adrian Burk was my back judge. He knew the game. He had been
a great player, an All-American at Baylor, and had had many
years in the NFL as a player. He worked hard but occasionally let
his eyes and mind wander over to the stands. This particular
Thanksgiving Day game in Dallas I kept yelling to Burk to hang
in there and to stay in the ball game. I thought Adrian was looking at the stands more than usual. Maybe it was my imagination.

But I would have bet a turkey dinner on it. He kept staring. I don't know whether he was trying to spot his family or not.

It was the fourth quarter when the public address system blared out, "Today's attendance is seventy-five thousand four hundred seventy-three people. It's a new Cotton Bowl record. The management thanks you."

Though the game was on national television and all the time-outs are carefully programmed, I took one on myself. I stopped the game, yelled downfield, "Hey, Burk, come on up here, will you?"

Burk rushed over to me. He knew it had to be something important I had to tell him. I had stopped the game and that was one thing Coach Lombardi hated any official to do. Burk reached me real fast. "What do you want?"

I looked at Burk. "Adrian, they say there are seventy-five thousand four hundred seventy-three people in the stands. Is that the count you got?"

Burk got the message. He was right on the ball with some great calls the last two minutes. That's when it's tough and a bit binding. A real nice guy. And a good official.

Even if Adrian occasionally let his eyes wander toward the stands, he was a delight to have on the crew. He kept everyone loose. Never took himself too seriously and would needle anyone who did. In addition to that, he was an excellent official and came up with the big call when it counted. The thing that I particularly enjoyed about Burk was his keen sense of humor.

Our crew was in Green Bay for a big one. We had dinner at the country club the Saturday night before the game. I looked over the room and spotted Ron Gibbs, a former referee and at that time a League observer of officials. He was having dinner with his wife.

I mentioned it to the fellows. "Oh, there's Ron Gibbs. I imagine he is the observer tomorrow. You all know him, don't you?"

Adrian Burk said, "Yeah, I know him. I remember him well. I was quarterbacking for the Eagles at the time and was knocked on my ass about thirty times that ball game. Roughed too. Not once did Gibbs throw his flag. He always looked at me and said, 'Get up, son. They never laid a hand on you.' I was on the ground all day. At least it seemed that way."

On the way out of the dining room, we stopped at Gibbs's table.

I spoke with him. "Ron, you know all the fellows, don't you?"

He looked at Burk and said, "I know all the others. But I don't recognize him."

Burk put out his hand and said, "Maybe if I lay down on the ground, you'll recognize me."

After any controversial call, especially against the home team, fans start growling and asking one another, "Where the hell did they find that official?"

You just don't find a pro football official. You look for him. The League office has come a long way in selecting their officials. They work at it the same way football teams do when they evaluate players. Men are scouted, evaluated and selected after years of having their work observed. Along with observers' verbal and written reports, the films of games that officials have worked in college are studied. There is no easy road to the top in any profession, least of all in pro football officiating. When the time comes for a man to get selected, he has worked hundreds of high school games and a major college scheduled before large crowds. He has been tested. For many years. Sometimes it doesn't work out, and the man selected lasts only a year or two. The turnover is not too high, but the total number of officials is not too high either.

At the present time during the football season there are 14 games every weekend. Seven officials at each game. That means 98 officials are used each weekend. The League carries an extra crew, and one crew is off each week.

A few years back Baltimore was at Washington late in the season for a nationally televised game. I particularly remember the game for it was so bitterly cold. The Redskins were having their problems. Our crew had a swing man, Tom Hensley, working in place of our regular head linesman, Burl Toler. It was Hensley's first year in the League and he was learning. Fast. At the two-minute warning I walked over to Otto Graham, the Washington coach, to advise him, "Two minutes left in the game, Coach." Just then a fan, slightly under the weather, ran out on the field right at Tom Hensley. Hensley had just called a holding penalty against the Redskins. Good call too. Not a tough call, as it was out in the open. I even saw it.

The fan kept coming at Hensley. When he got close enough, he threw a punch which Hensley ducked. Then Hensley swung his right and set the fan on his ass. A clean knockout. I ran up to Hensley and told him, "Tom, I don't know whether the League ever explained to you what a swing man is. You're not supposed to swing at a fan."

Hensley nodded and kept rubbing the knuckles of his right hand. He grinned at me. "Do you think I should have thrown my flag at him? I couldn't tell what team he was rooting for. He could have been for either side. The way I've been calling them, he had his choice."

Hensley is now one of the fine umpires in the League. And just as nice as ever. One-Punch Hensley. Good man to have on your side if you have to fight your way back to the locker room.

Hensley had been the swing man for Burl Toler. Toler was the first black to work as a professional football official. In fact, I believe he was the first black to work on any professional officiating level. Toler was no Johnny-come-lately in the business. He had been a great player with the University of San Francisco when they were tops in the country. They had people like Ollie Matson, Gino Marchetti, Dick Stanfel, Bob St. Clair and so many others who went into professional football. Nine of their first team jumped right into the pro ranks as players. Joe Kuharich was the coach and Pete Rozelle was their publicity man. Pretty good talent, wouldn't you say? Kuharich went on to coach in the pros with Washington and the Eagles.

The first regular League game that Burl Toler worked was on our crew and it was in Washington, D.C. There was pressure on him. Great pressure, for it was just after the Watts riots in 1965. The country was keeping one eye on the national scene and probably one eye on the football field. And on Toler.

Toler dressed or undressed by himself in a corner of our dressing room. He must have put on and removed his shoes a dozen times. I was wondering what to do to relax him. I just couldn't tell him, "Burl, relax. Forget you're the first black to work a professional game." He was smart. He knew people were watching. I kept trying to find a way to keep him loose. And was I ever lucky.

On Burl's twelfth time tying his shoelaces there was a knock on the dressing room door. Four black men were there. Three photographers and one reporter. The reporter asked for me.

"We have permission from Commissioner Rozelle to interview Mr. Toler. If it's all right with you. We're from *Ebony* magazine. We are doing a feature piece on Burl Toler for our readers."

I knew *Ebony* magazine was an excellent publication geared mainly for black readers. The request made sense. So did the article.

"What?" I asked. "Why Toler? He's just a rookie. The rest of us are veterans and never get asked for an interview. Why Toler?" I pretended to be annoyed, knowing full well the reasons.

"And," I continued, "did you know that Burl Toler is black?" I whispered that from behind the palm of my hand, but quite loudly. I wanted Burl to hear.

I heard a snap. Toler had broken his last shoelace. He was shaking his head. The newspaperman started to tell me all about *Ebony* magazine, but I waved him over to Toler. They did a great spread on Burl, as they do for most of their articles.

Toler was relaxed from then on.

Brad Pye, the excellent columnist for the *Los Angeles Sentinel*, the largest black-owned newspaper in the west, called me one day after Burl Toler had worked for a couple of games his first season.

"Norm," Pye asked, "what kind of an official is Toler?"

Without any hesitation I answered, "Brad, Toler would make it even if he were white."

Talk about your coincidences. Toler was hired as a football official in the NFL in the spring of 1965. A few months later the Watts riots broke out. I remember telling Burl, "Burl, didn't you pass the word along? Maybe they don't know you're hired. Or did they know? Maybe they're trying to tell us something."

The very first game Burl Toler worked was with me in a preseason game in Los Angeles right after the Watts riots. It was the *Los Angeles Times* charity game. It had been scheduled for a Saturday night, but the Coliseum area was still smoldering and burning. The game was postponed until the following Tuesday. It was the only game of its kind that I have ever worked or heard about. When I blew my whistle to start the game, I looked up into the stands of the Coliseum. Talk about rifles, belts and bayonets. There were National Guard soldiers standing at parade rest with their rifles, belts and bayonets every 15 feet in every aisle in the

Coliseum. I hoped they were on our side. Nothing happened in the ball game, and I don't even remember who won. I guess the officials won, for we all got out of there alive. That's what counts. Not the score. It isn't whether you win or lose, it's whether you make it to the dressing room.

Not too long ago I was the guest on a radio sports show, one in which the listeners call in and ask questions about professional football. Especially about a controversial call or two. It makes for an interesting hour. One listener, who seemed quite knowledgeable and was probably a high school football official, asked, "When is a man ready to work as a pro official?"

Without hesitation I answered, "After he has worked in the League for five years."

I wasn't being facetious. I was serious. Pro officiating is so different from college officiating. Don't misunderstand me. College officials are excellent. We refs in the pros all have come from the college ranks. It's just a different game. The adjustment from a more leisurely type of game to a more physical explosive game is tremendous. Every player in the pros has been the great star of his college team. There is no room for marginal players. Or for marginal officials. Sometimes the League makes a mistake in its selections of new officials, but not too often. The officials selected, just like the players, are the best in the country. Some are better than others, of course.

I remember a rules talk I gave to the Oakland Raiders a year or two ago. It was in their training camp in Santa Rosa. Ollie Spencer, who was Madden's top assistant for years, was upset about one of our officials. Probably called one against Oakland.

"Norm, he's not as good as the others. How come they aren't all the same? He doesn't seem to have as good judgment. We need consistency out there."

I hear that often. This time it bothered me. "Coach, I don't understand you. I know what you are saying. But it bothers me. Why the hell do all officials have to be the same? They're people. They work at their jobs. Look around this room. There are superstars. Guys making over a hundred thousand a year. There are players who are making fifty thousand a year and some guys are working for minimum. Some are faster, taller, heavier and better."

I then looked over at Coach Madden. He was enjoying all of it. "You know, Coach, there are some coaches who are better than others. They win more often."

I was safe. Madden was a big winner. And a great coach. I went on, "You guys kill me. Not now, please. Sit down, Upshaw. It was just an expression I used. What I am saying is that football officials are like everybody else. Some use better judgment, handle players better, gain respect easier, and are just better officials. Just like coaches and players. And just like other people. If you have two people doing a job, one is going to be better than the other. And one is going to be less good. Not worse, just less good. We just try to keep the ones not as good out of the League. There will always be a difference in officials. Someone has to be at the bottom of the ladder, no matter how short we make the ladder."

When the League is interested in a prospective football official, things are not left to chance. One of the League's observers, usually a former pro official who has retired (not been fired), watches the man work many times. Throughout the season. And the next season. Quite often, different observers will watch the man work. The observers spot-check a potential prospect on his judgment, reaction under pressure, decisiveness, game control and positioning. I throw in my criteria for a pro official. I always look to see if the prospect has the guts to call a foul against the home team with the clock running out and the game on the line. There's a difference when a foul is called. I call some of them safe fouls. You know, when neither team is hurt too much. I also look at his appearance. If he's heavy, write him off. He'll look like a ton on television. Especially in cold weather with all that extra clothing on.

If the reports are favorable and the observers think the prospect can handle the job, then one of the League's supervising officials tries to see him work. Art McNally, Jack Reader and Nick Skorich from the League office will give the man the once-over, and not too lightly. They also check with the pro officials who might be familiar with the man's ability and potential. If everything comes up to their standards, the man is given a series of psychological tests. (Fortunately, I got into the League before they gave those tests.) The man is then offered a contract. Quite often the active working officials tip the League office about prospective qualified officials. Many pro officials, by the nature of the occupation, are

especially friendly with college officials as they have worked together for years.

We're quite cautious in our evaluations. I learned to be careful
the hard way. I received a call from the League office one day
years ago. They were interested in some fellow from my section
of the country. The usual questions were asked, and finally the
big one.

"Norm, is he an official you think would make it in our league?"

"Yes, I do," I replied. "He's worth a contract. He's a good man."

"Fine," answered Mike Wilson, who was then Supervisor of
Officials. "We'll put him on your crew."

Without thinking, I shouted back, "Hey, wait a minute. I don't
think he's that good yet."

What I meant was, he had the potential to be a good official,
but let him learn with someone else. The prospect joined our crew
and is now one of the top officials in the country. In fact, he recently worked a Super Bowl game.

Many college officials check me frequently on how to go about
getting into the League. It isn't who you know. It's how good you
are, how you work and your experience. Quite often they want me
to recommend them. That's no problem, except when they are not
too good, but are friends.

"Hey, Norm. Can I use your name when I write to the NFL and
apply? It would be easier if I can say you told me to drop them
a note."

No problem. I have an understanding with the League office.
They are to check with me personally even though my name is
used as a reference. It means nothing to apply and say So-and-so
referred you. The big test is, Do you want him to be on your crew
when the chips are flying? A crew is only as good as its weakest
official. I keep that in mind all the time. I recommend only the
people I want out on the field with me in a tough situation. And
that happens dozens of times a ball game.

A pro official has traveled a long, hard and tough road. Lots of
bounces, bad calls (not too many or you would never get an application) and lots of good bounces. No one steps onto the football field as a pro official without having paid his dues. That's
working games for years. Most of our new officials have worked
big-time college games in front of large crowds. We get them

from every major conference in the country. Many of the men have been exposed to games in the Rose Bowl, Orange Bowl, Sugar Bowl and all the other bowl games. They have worked games at Notre Dame, Oklahoma, Nebraska, USC, Alabama, Penn State and all the top contenders. Before they even reach that level of football officiating, they have worked hundreds of high school games and junior college contests.

I had a solid background in officiating before I reached the NFL. I had worked literally hundreds of games. I had some high school officiating before joining the Marine Corps. After I got out, I worked high school and college games on the West Coast for eight more years before I finally heard from Bert Bell. During his era as Commissioner, there were no applications for applying to the NFL as there are today. It was a small enough league at that time to scout and check qualified officials personally.

I remember a neighbor of mine coming by my house. "Norm, are you moving, changing jobs or what?"

"Not that I know of. Why?"

"Well, some man was around running a check on you. He didn't want me to mention it to you. Said something about new insurance, but it sure didn't sound like insurance. He wanted to know if you gambled, chased, drank or were in any problem with the community. Don't know what kind of a policy you want."

I was pissed off. I wondered who the hell was checking me out. And why. Later on I found out that the League office had a former FBI man check me out as a prospective official. Of course, I hadn't known that I was a prospect at the time. It was only after I passed the check that I was even asked. Wouldn't it be a hell of a note if you had a neighbor who was mad at you and happened to be the one they asked? You would never get into the League.

A few years ago a well-dressed man of about 35 to 40 came into my office. We shook hands, and he gave me his card. He was the owner of a precision-tool firm. It was a good-sized company. It had to be for me to have heard of it.

I said to him, "It's nice to meet you. But I don't need any precision tools."

He laughed. "No, no. I don't want to sell you tools. I just gave you the card to identify myself. I'll come right to the point."

Before he did, I motioned to a chair and he sat down. So did I. He continued, "I've watched you work out on the football field.

I also have watched the other men work. I'd like to become a National League referee. It looks like fun and not too tough, and I love to travel."

I looked at him. What the hell did he mean, he watched me work and thought he could handle the job!

"What you need to do is to drop Art McNally a letter telling him you're interested, and he'll mail you a letter with an application form," I advised him.

The man nodded. "I've done all that and have his letter. I'm having trouble filling it out."

"What do you mean, trouble? Just list your answers and include your major college schedule of games for this year and mention last year's schedule."

"Well, I've never worked any major college games."

"That's okay. List the small college games you've worked, or even the junior college games."

"I've never worked those either."

I didn't say anything for a few seconds. I wanted to be kind, and besides it was a League affair. I finally said, "Send him your high school football schedule then if you haven't done anything else."

"I've never worked any high school games either."

"Did you ever officiate anywhere?"

"Sure I did. I worked the bases in the Little League baseball where my kids play."

I suggested that he join the local Football Officials Association, start working high school games and come up from there. Perhaps in later years he could legitimately apply. The League would like a prospect to have 10 years' experience in officiating football, at least five of which has to be on a varsity college level. The age span of candidates should be in the range of 32 to 44 years of age. That will enable the League to get at least 10 good years out of a new man.

A new referee in the National Football League has to watch himself. The game is so fascinating, the caliber of play so outstanding and the people so very professional that a new man can get into trouble very quickly. It is easy to become complacent, watch the game, and forget what you are supposed to do out on the field.

Bud Brubaker, one of the fine officials, and I were talking to a new referee one day during the season. Innocently, I asked him, "How are you going? How do you like it?"

He smiled and said, "Great. I'm enjoying it. It's a ball."

Brubaker looked at me and said, "Did anybody ever ask you to dance, Norm?"

The new referee got the word.

Today's pro football officials come from all parts of the country and all walks of life. They are all successful men in their chosen professions. Their breadth of experience is varied, their one common interest football. Many of them have played college and pro football and have coached on the different levels of competition; they become referees to stay in football. They are college graduates, though this is not a League requirement.

Remember Hugh McElhenny? Hustling Hugh of the 49ers. I was one of the coaches when he was in our high school. Sometimes during a game I refereed for San Francisco when he was a pro and was running wild, I would get a wee bit embarrassed. After McElhenny was tackled and downed, I would reach for the ball. Invariably, he would look up at me and say, "Hi, Coach. How's Charlotte and the boys?"

I would whisper real fast, "Not here, Mac, not here. Ask me after the game." The other team kept wondering who the hell Charlotte was. To say nothing about the boys.

McElhenny was one of the two best running backs that I have ever seen in the National Football League. The other one was Gale Sayers of the Chicago Bears. I saw Sayers do things out on the field that I couldn't believe. One afternoon in Chicago I saw Gale Sayers put on the greatest exhibition of open field running that I have ever seen. And I have seen most of the great ones. At least in the past 25 years. It was in Wrigley Field against the San Francisco 49ers one misty, muggy day. Sayers scored six touchdowns. Six. If Halas had let him play longer, he would have had three more scores. It was fantastic. And so was he.

If I weren't the referee and out on the field that day and had not seen it firsthand, I would have thought it was a setup for a movie. The 49er players kept dropping off him when they tried to tackle him. He swerved and swirled all over that wet field.

The third quarter ended just as Sayers ran a punt back about 40 yards. Sayers stumbled and a 49er player was able to down him on his own 10-yard line. Larry Morris, who had rushed the punter, was lying on the ground close to me as we both watched Sayers do his dance downfield. Simply unbelievable. No one would touch him, but he stumbled.

Just as Sayers was tackled, the gun sounded to end the third quarter, Larry Morris turned to me, shook his head and said, "They had to shoot him to stop him."

We have officials who are lawyers, college professors, deans and registrars of universities, presidents of businesses, druggists, architects, superintendents of schools, principals of large secondary schools, district managers of steel corporations, directors of sales, full-time speakers, bank presidents, land developers, sales counselors, directors of athletics, insurance executives, sales managers of sporting goods companies, mechanical engineers and quite a number of Ph.D.s. One of them was even a State Senator from Texas. These are people who have had to make decisions, important ones, when it counts and with judgment.

What bugs me is that just about every person who has ever seen a pro game thinks he could be a pro official. He won't believe that it takes years of hard work and sweat, with lots of good bounces and luck before you reach the big time. Football is a game of bounces. A good official needs good bounces. Sometimes it's better to be lucky than good. Things may move along smoothly for 59 minutes of a ball game and then—Bang! All hell breaks loose. It seems as if things that were bouncing right start to take that crazy bounce. It is then that experience and common sense make the pro official. Most people could learn the rule book even though it is over 100 pages of technical stuff. But it is the instantaneous call that makes the difference. There are no committee meetings, no films to review and no second chances when the call has to be made. It's bang-bang! Right now! During an average game an official will have to make 50 to 60 sudden decisions which could affect the outcome. There is no room for guesswork; there must be a decisive right call. Sometimes the decisive call is a no-call.

To be a good official, it pays to have a sense of humor. Besides, some very funny things are said out on the field. Quarterbacks and linebackers seem to have a better sense of humor than the others. Maybe it's because quarterbacks seldom run with the ball, and linebackers get to belt their opponents. Legally, of course. Most of the time anyway.

When you mention linebackers, Butkus jumps right out at you. Dick Butkus was the best middle linebacker that I have ever seen. And I have seen all the great ones in the past twenty-odd years. That's just when middle linebackers started to come into their own. Butkus was overpowering. He completely dominated the game.

I have never seen Butkus have a bad day. He intimidated teams by his ability. He was a hard player, nothing dirty about him at all. He was active all the time. He put in a full week's work every Sunday afternoon. It was not playtime for him. And he took his lumps as well as dishing it out. Never complained. At least not too much. He was the best at his position. No question about it.

The Chicago Bears, along with Dick Butkus, were playing Miami in the Orange Bowl. For some unknown reason a fight broke out between Dick Evey of the Bears and Larry Little of the Dolphins. It was a good one too. Dick Butkus tried to break it up by grabbing Little from the rear in a bear hug. Ralph Morcroft, the umpire, also tried to break it up by grabbing Butkus from the rear in a bear hug. Picture that if you can: Evey trying to get at Little, Butkus bear-hugging Little from the rear, and the umpire, Morcroft, bear-hugging Butkus from the rear. Morcroft kept pulling Butkus backward. You guessed it. They all fell down backward with Morcroft on the bottom of the pile, with Butkus, Little and Evey on top of him and one another. Morcroft reached up and grabbed Butkus' face mask to keep him from getting up. One of Morcroft's fingers went in too far under the face mask. Butkus bit it. Probably thought it was an opponent's finger. Come to think about it, some people think that's what we officials are!

Morcroft's finger was bitten to the bone. He was bleeding profusely. The blood stopped the fight. Three stitches closed the wound. Morcroft unloaded five players from the game. Was he ever bitter!

A sports writer from the *Miami Herald* wrote in his column the next morning, "Up at the dog track the canines behaved beautifully. But at the Orange Bowl a man bit a man."

A year later I was back in Chicago to work a game. Something happened which irritated Butkus. I didn't like to irritate Butkus. But here he was in front of me, talking and waving his finger at me. He was unhappy about a call and was letting me know. He kept talking and pointing his finger at me for emphasis.

"Butkus," I said, "if you don't stop waving that finger at me, I'll bite your head off."

He changed his tune and answered, "If you do, you'll have more brains in your stomach than in your head."

You know, he may have been right. Funny thing. I was reading Carl Sandburg's *Abraham Lincoln* shortly after that game and discovered that Lincoln had said the same thing about some politician. Nice to know football players read. Especially middle linebackers.

When I mention outstanding middle linebackers, I have to speak out and say Ray Nitschke. I've seen him have as good a day as Butkus, but he was not the intimidating factor that Butkus was. Awfully close though. Maybe right there.

One year in late November I got on a plane in Los Angeles for Green Bay one Saturday morning. It was 75 degrees when I left Los Angeles. And it was 17 degrees when I got off the plane in Green Bay late that Saturday afternoon. And me with a short-sleeve shirt and a thin topcoat.

Sunday afternoon wasn't much better. Or warmer. I think it was in the low 20's when I went to the center of the field for the coin toss. I felt terrible. The weather had gotten to me. My legs were aching, my nose was stuffed, and my throat was raspy.

Ray Nitschke, captain of the Packers, was standing in the middle of the field, waiting for the Bears' captain. I was standing with him. Nitschke watched me blow my nose. He asked me, "What's wrong, Norm? Don't you feel good?"

I blew again. And again. "I don't know what's wrong, Ray. My legs ache, my nose is stuffed and I think I have a cold or something in my head."

Nitschke looked at me. "It must be a cold in your head, Norm. I'm sure you don't have anything else there."

I wonder why he didn't laugh when he said that.

Ray Nitschke was tough, and mean! Not dirty—just tough and mean.

My Achilles tendon had been acting up. It hurt like hell. I had it taped before every game. Usually by the home team trainer. As I was in Green Bay, I walked over to their training room to get my heel taped. All the team trainers were glad to do it, just as long as I worked it in between the players' taping.

Nitschke was on the training table as I got to the door of the training room, still wearing my street clothes. The guard at the door stopped me and asked, "What do you want?"

I looked at the guard and said, "I want to get my Achilles taped."

The guard nodded. "Are you with television?"

"No, I'm not. Are they taping the announcers now?"

Nitschke laughed. He waved me in, rolled off the table and said, "Jump up on the table, Norm. Show me if you can move fast enough to be able to get up and down the field. I don't believe what the other guys say."

Quite often the television fans and the stadium spectators see the players and the referee talking. The dialogue varies, but basically it's the same routine with a different switch. Players wonder, Why the penalty? since they don't commit any fouls. They are serious, believe me. So am I. An official better not laugh on the field. No one appreciates it. Big men are bashing one another, and it ain't funny, although something happens that we milk for a laugh to break the tension.

Remember Frank Ryan? An outstanding quarterback. First with the Los Angeles Rams and then with the Cleveland Browns. Won a world championship with the Browns. He's now the director of athletics at Yale University. That's Dr. Ryan. I just saw a news item about him the other day in the papers.

I remember one game in Cleveland. I was taped live for a segment on "Countdown to Touchdown," a CBS show featuring Tom Harmon. One of my sons recently had occasion to play the tape, and I laughed again.

Frank Ryan, the Cleveland quarterback, had just received his doctorate in higher mathematics. His dissertation had an unpronounceable thesis. I couldn't even get the letters in the proper place.

It was second down and nine when Ryan handed off to Jim Brown. Brown went off tackle for seven yards. The Colts were off side on the play. That meant an option for Cleveland.

"Hey, Ryan, you have an option. Listen to it. Look over to the bench, if you need help. You made seven yards, so it will be third and two to go. Or if you take the offside penalty, it will be second and four to go. Got it?"

"Wait a minute, Norm. Take it easy. Slow it down. How do you get four to go?" Ryan asked as he looked over toward the bench.

"Well, Doctor Ryan, it's like this. You start with nine and take away five. That leaves four. In the Los Angeles city schools we call that remedial math."

Ryan called me something else. He smiled though. His doctorate almost blew the option.

During that game I had to throw my penalty flag on Leroy Kelly, an excellent runner for the Browns. He moved too quickly. In other words, he missed the count and started forward a half step too soon before the ball was snapped. That's illegal motion. Kelly liked to get that extra half step before he took the hand-off. An outstanding player with or without that extra half step. Ryan came up to me and said, "Norm, we work on coordinating that hand-off. Take a good look at it. It's legal. Kelly is fast. He goes one way, comes back and I hand off to him. We try to correlate the hand-off and his move."

At least that's what I thought he said. I looked at Ryan and said, "Frank, when you say correlate, do you mean you work together?"

Ryan stared at me. He didn't know if I was pulling his leg or not. Connell, my umpire, came up and asked, "What'd he say?"

Ryan was still with me. "I don't know, Joe. He said correlate. Is that a dirty word? Should I throw the flag for swearing? I guess not. Let's play ball. That's five yards for illegal motion, correlating or not."

The world championship game the Baltimore Colts had in Cleveland was one that I will not forget. At the end of the first half I asked Frank Ryan, the Cleveland captain, if he wanted to kick off to start the second half or to receive the ball. It was a windy day and passes were floating all over the place. A decision had to be made. Did Cleveland want the wind in the third or fourth quarter? Ryan looked at me, then walked over to Blanton Collier, the Browns' head coach. Nick Skorich, the assistant coach, was standing next to Collier. There we were, the four of us, wait-ing for a decision. Finally, I forced the issue. I spoke to Collier.

"Coach, what do you want to do—kick off or receive?"

He looked at Ryan. "What do you want to do, Frank? What do you think? Should we take the wind now or in the fourth quarter?"

Ryan wasn't about to make the choice. He looked back at Col-lier and said, "You're the coach. Tell me what you want me to do."

Skorich glanced over at me. Then he looked at Collier and Ryan. Skorich shrugged his shoulders and said, "Hell, we'll kick off that way."

That's what they did. And it was an excellent decision. Cleve-land won easily by a score of 27–0. The next day, when I left Cleveland to return to Los Angeles, I read the Cleveland sports pages. There was a two-column spread about the strategy used in the second half regarding the wind factor. The big thing was the way the coaching staff had it all planned what to do if they had the option the second half. You know—the wind and all that stuff.

Sure they did! It took two questions and what-the-hell shrug of the shoulders, and that's strategy. It worked too.

No one realizes it, but that game was shortchanged 27 seconds. It was the only way to go. At that time the back judge kept the of-ficial time of the game. The scoreboard clock was not the official time then, as it is today. Time was kept on the field. With 27 sec-onds to play, the fans in Cleveland Stadium (which is one of the coldest places to work, as the wind comes right off Lake Erie) broke from the stands and ran onto the field. They were all over the sidelines and behind the end lines. I was worried that some-one would get hurt if a runner went out of bounds. I knew that I couldn't get them back into the stands. If the game had been close, I wouldn't have had any choice but to stop the game and get the fans off the field. But it was 27–0 with only 27 seconds left to play.

I yelled over to Tom Kelleher, a top-notch official, to shoot his gun. One of the players looked up at the scoreboard clock and saw 27 seconds big as life. He said, "Hey, there's still time left on the clock."

Just then Kelleher shot the gun which ended the game. I looked at the player and told him, "No, there isn't. The game is over."

There were still 27 seconds left on the clock. With the score 27–0 in favor of the Browns and no one going anywhere, it made sense. And I didn't want anyone to get hurt. We can't do that now, for the official time is kept on the scoreboard clock. Life goes on. But I'm ahead of the game by 27 seconds.

Football refereeing has its perks. Like the time I got three days' pay working in the movie *The Fortune Cookie*. It starred Jack Lemmon and Walter Matthau. Billy Wilder was the director.

I had refereed the ball game in Cleveland that Sunday. The movie company planned to use the actual game footage of the game I worked. They would dub in the shots with Jack Lemmon the following three days in the Cleveland Stadium. Lemmon played the role of a photographer who was bowled over at the sideline as he was taking a picture. The Cleveland runner ran a wide sweep and was forced out of bounds. Right into Jack Lemmon. Lemmon pretended to be seriously injured. That allowed Walter Matthau, his lawyer, to sue the Cleveland Browns and also the city of Cleveland. It was a fraudulent insurance scam.

My job was to get the player (who felt responsible for knocking Jack Lemmon down) back into the ball game. The game had to go on. I ran over to the sideline, where Lemmon was flat on his back. Out. The runner (a real actor in the dubbed shots) hovered over Lemmon anxiously. All I had to say was seven words. Two simple sentences. "Let's play. Get back to your huddle."

Not too tough. Right? I blew the lines. All two of them. I didn't know it then, but I was cut out of the picture.

The one time I gave a good reading of my seven words, the director reminded me who the star was.

"Norm," he told me, "Don't stand in front of Jack."

To make the dubbed shots on Monday look realistic, they needed people in the stands. Especially for the shots of Jack Lemmon lying on the ground knocked out, with the player peering down at him. They would get the shot of Lemmon and the crowd in the background. A notice in the morning paper brought out 5,000 fans. They were allowed in free to see the filming, and were seated in one section. As the assistant director was setting up the day's shooting schedule, his assistants tried to keep the 5,000 fans happy. They had raffles, prizes and introductions until the actual shooting began. The Browns' TV announcer, Ken Coleman, did a great job of keeping things moving and quiet. He introduced the entire cast. Each introduction was preceded by a few kind remarks about the actor's ability. The fans were enthusiastic. Especially when Jack Lemmon took a bow. Then it was my turn. Coleman didn't get more than my name out when the place erupted. I never heard such booing. All Coleman said was "And Norm Schachter." That undid all the goodwill the prizes and souvenirs had bought.

Sometimes the conversation I have with the players on the field carries over to the dressing room. I steer clear of anyone who might still be bitter. But sometimes I can't help myself. Minnesota had just lost a tough ball game to the Packers. After the game, and after I had finished showering and dressing, I walked out of our dressing room. I went to the phone booth right by the door. I wanted to say good-bye to a friend in Green Bay. I reached for a dime but had only four quarters. Just then, Fran Tarkenton walked out of his dressing room and came toward me. I yelled, "Hey, Francis, do you have change for a quarter?"

Fran looked at me and asked, "What do you need?"

"I need a dime, Francis. I want to call a friend."

"Here's two dimes. Call all your friends."

Believe me, there are no happy losers. Only bitter ones.

Quite often we referees get to have some conversation with the front office people. They are smart. They wouldn't have their jobs if they weren't. They know their business, and also realize how significant a contribution the officials make to the success of the game. Their attitude toward the third team is wholesome and decent. I can't say enough about any of them, and that also goes for the owners. Oh, sometimes one of the owners will fly off the handle, but that's just after a tough loss of a ball game. A day or so later he realizes he was upset, and says something differently. I have found that a general manager's attitude and behavior key off the owner's behavior and attitudes.

Don Kellett was general manager of the Baltimore Colts for many years. He was one helluva guy. One year I had a "crucial" in Baltimore. It was for first place and a must-win for both teams. Chicago was in Baltimore and all tickets were gone. My brother-in-law was stationed at the Pentagon and called me about buying a couple of tickets. I never have gotten into the ticket business. However, I hadn't seen him for years, so I wrote Don Kellett and enclosed my check.

My check was returned with a note advising me that two tickets would be left at the will-call window. And, "Norm, the day I ever charge a referee for tickets is the day I quit the business." They didn't come any nicer then Don Kellett.

As things so often happen, one of my calls really hurt the Colts. It was a foul, and when a referee makes the call he has to make, it becomes his call or foul. That's the business. And we get it.

I was walking out to the parking lot after the game. And who should I run smack into? You guessed it. It was Don Kellett. He walked by me, turned back and said, "Norm, I should have charged you double for those tickets."

It's tough to lose. But I think he was kidding. I hope.

Baltimore's Memorial Stadium was jumping—all over me. I stood in the center of the field, listening to the howls and groans of the capacity crowd of over 60,000. Bert Jones, the Colts' fine quarterback, had just been bowled over. Legally. That's what I thought. No one else did though. I was catching hell. Jones rushed me. Not only did he move quickly, but his mouth was moving just as fast.

"Didn't you see him rough me? He almost tore my head off."

I waited until Jones finished the quarterback's pledge. When he was within a yard of me, I raised my hand in a "How" salute.

"How's your dad feeling?"

That stopped him. "What? What did you say? How's my dad? Fine. Why?"

"He sure was one helluva ballplayer. One of the best Cleveland ever had. Great hands. Fine receiver. Never said a word to me, or any other official all the years he was with the Browns. Never said a word about being held or roughed. Just did his job and let me do mine. Dub Jones was a great competitor. Be sure to say hello for me."

Bert Jones smiled, nodded and ran back to his huddle.

The first year New Orleans played in the Superdome, they had a pre-season game against Denver. There was a holding penalty against New Orleans. I was explaining the option to the Denver captain. We were standing under the six-sided replay screen which is 10 yards long on all six sides. It is suspended from the rafters and hangs over the center of the field. It weighs over eight tons. It's big, all right. You have to see it to believe it.

As I was explaining the option, the Denver captain asked me to move away from under the large, heavy replay screen. "Would you mind moving away from beneath this screen? I understand that it was built by the low bidder," he said, as we both moved away.

He gets my vote for All-Pro.

In that game I had a little conversation with Bill Van Heusen, the Denver punter. The Denver Broncos play their home games at the Denver Mile High Stadium. It is a mile above sea level. The air is thinner and it moves around quite a bit. Van Heusen, Denver's punter and a good one, knows how to adjust for the wind factor, especially in his home stadium. The wind there changes suddenly and quickly. In the Superdome in New Orleans, Van Heusen had a different problem. There was no wind.

The second time Denver had to punt, Van Heusen turned to me as we were both back in our respective positions. He stood about 14 yards deep and I was off to his right about four yards to check possible running into the kicker. "You know," he said, "this place may be tough to kick in. There are no wind pockets, currents or movements. On my last punt, I thought the ball fluttered a little. Maybe I was kicking against their air conditioning? What do you think?"

I didn't answer. It's a good thing I didn't. He booted the hell out of the ball, air conditioning or not.

The one time that I wished I had a yo-yo for a flag was in San Diego. It would have been back in my hand before it had hit the ground. It was on a try attempt after a touchdown. The try was wide and the play was over. But I threw my flag anyway as a San Diego player ran into the place-kick holder. Running into the holder is not a foul, unless it is unnecessary roughness. The try may have been over, but the conversation lingered on.

Steve Zabel, captain of the Eagles, ran up to me. "Your flag is down. We want the penalty and a rekick."

"No way, Zabel. No foul and no rekick," I said very quickly. I wanted to get away from it.

"What do you mean, no foul? I see a flag on the ground. It's yours, isn't it? I've never heard or seen this before," he said as he followed me.

"Listen. You've been around a long time. You claim that you have never heard of such a thing. You claim that you've never seen such a thing. Think how lucky you are today. For the first time in your life, you're not only going to see it, but you're going to hear it. No penalty."

With that I bent down and picked up the flag. I straightened up real fast. I had too much exposed.

Instant replay has made the officials look better than ever. It also has made it easier for the fan to second-guess us. But you have to remember that I don't get any instant replay to help me make the call. There's no second look. Maybe there should be. And I'm sure that down the road sometime there will be. Right now, it's bang-bang. And throw the flag. Or keep it in your pocket. I honestly believe that instant replay is a blessing for the officials. Now we don't have to defend our every call. Just a few of them. The call is right there. Right on film. Over and over again. It doesn't ever change.

We have to work very closely with television. Each time-out is worth lots of dollars. If we miss too many time-outs, I think we would miss working. I remember a championship game in Chicago one year. It was the last time the Bears won the title. There was little scoring in the first half. At that time we gave television time-outs only after a score or on a regular team time-out. It's different now, of course. It's all programmed today. Each television spot runs into big figures.

At the end of the first half we had taken only three time-outs for television. They were hurting. We were short four television time-outs. It was a problem.

Ski, the CBS producer, stormed into the dressing room at half time, shouting, "Norm, you owe me a half million dollars."

I offered him a cup of coffee. "Don't worry, Ski, I'll pay it back this next half."

I did too. Who worries about a half million dollars?

Just a quick word about television and its time-outs. And how we take those time-outs for television commercials. Thats' a big,

big business. Each time-out is worth a small fortune. Super Bowl time-outs go for $550,000 apiece. That's for a one-minute commercial. Or around that. Regular season games with their time-outs don't bring that much, of course. There's not that large a television audience. We signal TV to go for its commercials after a score, after an injury to a player who will require more than a minute to leave the game, or after a change of possession. It's nice if you can have both teams have an offensive series before you call the first TV time-out. But sometimes that's tough to do. We never kill the clock for television within the 20-yard line when a team is driving for a score. We don't want to stop their momentum.

I remember Johnny Unitas in his last year or so with the Baltimore Colts. He threw short swing passes and handed off for 12 minutes of the first quarter in a game with the Jets and Namath. He kept the ball and ate up the time. And—no injuries and no time-outs and no television commercials. I was sweating and watching the TV man on the sideline who waved his hands continuously for 8 of those 12 minutes when Unitas kept the ball. Look over at the 20- or 25-yard sideline the next time you see a game. See if you can spot the TV man who works with the referee. There's no problem on regular team time-outs or on an injury. They're automatic. The TV man on the sideline might be wearing a red hat or red coat or have another recognizable piece of clothing, anything which will stand out and enable the referee to spot him and pick him up. When television wants a time-out for a commercial, the TV relay man on the sideline folds both arms across his chest. That tips me, as a referee, that they want a time-out. I then know he needs one and wants one. I then point to the ground, which tells him that I am aware of his needs. The first chance that I get—whether it's a change of possession after a kick or a score—I call time out and touch my cap, which indicates that it's a referee's time-out. I then hold my arms straight out to the sides. Television then goes into its commercial. The television relay man on the sideline then holds one arm across his chest. That indicates to me that he is on the air with a commercial. When he drops his arm, I blow my whistle to start the game again. We try to give them four TV commercials in the first quarter, five in the second quarter, five in the third quarter and five in the fourth quarter. One of the TV time-outs in the second and fourth quarters comes at the two-minute warning we give the coaches. We always stop the game then. (Incidentally, we have some different timing rules for the last two minutes of a half. It's important to notify the head coach at that time. He usually rearranges his plans. Or better yet, he goes to his planned routine for the last two minutes. Look at those hurry-up offenses in the last two minutes when a team is behind. It's amazing how many plays they get in. It makes a fan wonder why they don't use the two-minute hurry-up offense all game long. That's what some fans think. I hear it often.)

I always have needled the network people when they come into the dressing room to introduce the television relay man on the sideline. It seems as if they change them frequently. All three networks—CBS, NBC, ABC—spend fortunes in televising the football games. Then they often get some local person, often without training, to stand on the sideline to key the whole operation. I've told them, "Hell, you spend millions and get millions and you get a guy you either give a couple of tickets or pay him practically nothing to key the whole damn thing. Shit, if I ran my job out on the field that way, the game would never get off the ground." ABC does have one man who works all Monday night football games. He's always the same man on the sideline.

I remember one time in New York at Yankee Stadium. We had a TV relay man on the sideline on a nationally televised game who kept fouling us up. Before the game they brought him into our dressing room to get him briefed. We have enough to do besides go through snapping in a new man with a few choice words like "Now remember. When you need a TV commercial time-out, fold both arms across your chest. And when you're on the air with that commercial, just drop one of the two arms and keep one arm across your chest."

The man nodded, repeated what I said and went out and fouled up the whole operation. On national TV.

He got his signals mixed up. When he was on live with a commercial, he had both arms folded across his chest. When he needed a commercial, he put one arm across his chest. Everything was ass-backwards. Once he went on without any warning. It upset me, for I had enough problems with the game. Some people tell me, "with every game." I went over several times to the sideline and told him the proper procedure again. But he was still confused. I didn't blame him. He was a spectator with a good

deal and forgot what he was out on the field for. He became
personally involved with the Giants moving the ball. I didn't
hear him cheer for the Giants, but he sure did get enthusiastic
on their successful plays. I finally had all I could take, so I went
over and told him, "Next time buy a ticket and sit in the stands."

The next thing I heard was Fette yelling, "Hey, Norm, you're
on your own. The sideline man just quit. He walked off the field."

I didn't believe it. No one had ever done that before. I looked
over and sure enough, there was a headset on the ground, with
the red hat and no one under it. He did just quit. We got them all
of their TV commercial time-outs. But it was touch and go. And
he did go.

Don't misunderstand me. The TV announcers, producers and
directors are as professional as the players. More so. Some are better prepared, some have deeper insights into the flow of the game
and some are just better. I imagine they are also like people. It's
interesting how announcers differ though. Some come to the
officials' dressing room to visit, check signals and talk football.
Others we never see, which is just as well. We get reports on what
they say though. Nine out of ten TV announcers understand the
problems of officials. They try not to second-guess, but not always.
When they see the instant replay and there is a mistake (and we
make them, but not too often), some really go to town on us. It's
easy then.

Ray Scott has been a friend for many years. We go back to the
time he was the Green Bay announcer during their great years.
He is an outstanding television and radio announcer. He also
helped me more than my eye doctor. He cured me once and for
all. The eye doctor never helped me at all.

I wore contact lenses years ago. That's when I was interested in
seeing. However, I had trouble. Lots of trouble. I guess it was my
own fault, for I didn't wear them long enough to get used to
them. One or both lenses would slip off the pupils of my eyes during the ball game. It was difficult to know whether the contact
lenses were in place or not. I had my own test to check whether I
could see deep or not.

From my referee's position 10 yards or so behind the quarterback, I would place my right palm over my right eye. Then I
would look at the scoreboard. If I could see the time listed on the
board, I knew I was ready for the long field goal. I knew the lens

was in place. Then I would change hands. I would use my left palm to cover my left eye. I would use the same test. If I could see the time listed on the scoreboard, I would pass my eye test. If not, I knew I would need help in finding the lost lens in my eye. I would get that help during half time in our dressing room. I was not about to have one of those big linemen with their large fingers poke around my eye with big muddy hands. Can you hear the crowd if they saw that?

Ed Marion, the head linesman, also wore contact lenses. He never had any problems. He'd watch me go through my routine of hand over eye. When I took my hand down and looked over at Marion, he would mimic my moves.

Ray Scott, a real pro, came to the officials' dressing room one Sunday prior to kickoff. He walked over to me. "Norm, I did your game for TV last week on CBS. You threw me a curve all afternoon. I noticed the new signal, but can't find it in the rule book. No one in the booth had seen it before. Is it a new one? What's the hand-over-the-eye signal?"

I forgot to thank Ray Scott. After his question, I got rid of those damn contact lenses. I never felt as good, though I don't think I saw as well.

Funny how I stop to think of all the players I've known over a couple of decades. Most ballplayers do tend to fade away. At least fade away from my thoughts, except for an occasional story. Most of them drop out with memories and injuries. A few have become coaches. And some have become television and radio announcers. Players like Gifford, Meredith, Merlin Olsen, Brodie, Jurgensen, Pat Summerall, Tom Brookshier, Jim Hill and so many more are still around. At least up in the TV booth someplace in the country on Sunday afternoons during football season. Those are the ones that I see more often. Just like players and officials. Some are better than others. Monty Stickles is one of them who stays active, especially around the San Francisco area. I still chuckle over my first contact with him. Usually his contacts are nothing to laugh about, especially those he had on the football field.

Joe Kuharich had just assumed the job of Supervisor of Officials for the NFL. The previous year he had coached at Notre Dame. Before then, he had done a nice job with the Washington Redskins. Later on, he coached the Eagles. He knew football from all angles. When he took over the job as supervisor, he decided to go with me when I made my rules talks to the various teams.

Kuharich and I visited the San Francisco 49ers training camp. It was held at St. Mary's College of California at Moraga. It was my yearly visit to the training camp to review rules, old ones and the new ones.

Red Hickey was coach of the 49ers. He met Joe and me when we reached the 49er camp. He took us to the dining room. As the three of us were talking, Monty Stickles, who had graduated from Notre Dame the previous year and had been everybody's All-American, drove up in a nice car. He was a rookie with the 49ers and had been a high draft choice. Kuharich had been his coach at Notre Dame.

Before we could shake hands, Red Hickey turned to Kuharich and put the needle to him. "Hey, Joe, I hear Stickles took a pay cut to come into the NFL from Notre Dame. Is that true?"

Stickles and Kuharich both laughed. They must hear that song all the time. So do other big-time college coaches, I'm sure. But not anymore with the salaries they're paying today in the pros.

Stickles had some excellent years in the pros. A helluva ball-player. When he played, things happened. Monty Stickles is now a fine announcer and sports-talk host on radio in San Francisco. He did a lot of talking out on the field as a player, so he had excellent training for his radio job. Stickles was a tough tight end for the 49ers. Players kept an eye on him. So did I.

After a rough afternoon in San Francisco's Kezar Stadium, I was waiting for a taxi outside the stadium. My wife was with me, as was Burl Toler. Suddenly I felt this bang across my back. Without turning around, I said, "Stickles, knock it off. Keep your hands to yourself."

"How did you know it was me, Norm? Your back was to me."

"Listen, Monty, I watched you all afternoon on the field. Who the hell else could it be at Kezar or in San Francisco?"

Stickles laughed, and off he went. I never did tell him that I had spotted him coming toward me out of the corner of my eye.

Not too long ago after a controversial game in Oakland, the reporters and radio people were waiting outside the Oakland Raiders' dressing room. I had just finished refereeing the game against New England. As I was walking to the dressing room, I spotted Monty Stickles and his co-announcer. Stickles was doing the color.

When I got close to them, Monty's co-worker yelled, "Hey, Norm. I thought they said you had retired last year."

Before I could answer, my good friend Stickles pops up, "No, that wasn't what they said. They said he should have retired."

Maybe they were right!

Someone asked me not too long ago to list qualities that a successful referee in the NFL must have.

No problem. Hell, I've thought about what makes a successful referee (or any official) for over 25 years. They are qualities that are basically the same as for success in any other business or profession.

Have a sense of humor. Be able to laugh at yourself. Don't take yourself too seriously. Take the job seriously, but not yourself. If you don't, you won't be around long enough to have any laughs. In my office I have a blown-up, signed, autographed cartoon by Jim Berry, the syndicated cartoonist of "Berry's World," which hangs above my desk. It shows a referee in full uniform lying on a psychiatrist's couch with the psychiatrist saying, "When did you first suspect you were God?"

A pro referee can't fall into that trap. His actions, mannerisms and attitudes have to signify control of the game. But not in an autocratic, dictatorial manner. A referee doesn't handle players and coaches. You handle horses and dogs. No one pays to see the referee work the game. Not even his family. I remember when I first started to referee, I was quite enthusiastic and perhaps showboatish. My wife quickly reminded me, "If you were advertised to referee in the Coliseum, and the two teams didn't play, no one, not even me, would come out to watch you." Not even her!

It was at that time that I started to strive for anonymity. Television changed that in a hurry. Especially after a few controversial calls. For a while I thought my name was Hey You Sonavabitch.

The day a referee takes himself too seriously is the day he should put away his whistle, his striped shirt and short white knickers. That's the time he should grow up and put on a pair of long pants.

I had a game in Cleveland. I got on a plane from Los Angeles which flew directly to Cleveland. It was a light flight, very few passengers. I was reading A Smattering of Ignorance by Oscar Levant. When the stewardess finished serving breakfast to the three of us in the first cabin, she sat down next to me. I had worked the last Super Bowl game and the three previously nationally televised games. I figured everyone knew me.

She smiled at me. "Where are you going?"

That bothered me. It was a nonstop flight to Cleveland. I smiled and said, "Cleveland." Probably the only right call I'd make that weekend.

"Are you from Cleveland? What are you going to do there?" she asked me without waiting for any answers.

"I'm going to the football game. You see, I like football."

Finally, I stopped talking. She said, "What are you reading? What a pretty book cover."

It was. It was a polka-dot cover. She had never heard of Oscar Levant. But she loved that book cover.

I told her, "I'm coming back tomorrow night. I don't think I can catch your five-twenty P.M. flight. The game starts at two o'clock and I doubt if I can make it. I'll probably have to go through Chicago."

That didn't upset her.

I worked the game the next day. It ended earlier than I had thought it would. I caught the 5:20 P.M. flight to Los Angeles. As I entered the plane, the same stewardess was there, smiling. It was another light flight going back.

We had dinner and I settled down to finish my Oscar Levant book. The stewardess sat down next to me and—here we go again.

"Hi, there. What are you reading? What an attractive book cover on that book? May I see it, please?" she gushed.

I handed her the book and waited. She looked it over, turned to me and said, "This is the strangest coincidence. We had a man fly out yesterday who was reading the same book."

Oh, well! Fame is so fleeting.

An NFL football referee has to have his eyes examined once a year. I'm not sure that brain surgeons do. I'm positive that barbers don't. At least not my barber. Harry has cut my hair for many years. He likes football, and as he cuts, he talks football. He seems familiar with the players and my refereeing.

Just before last season I was in his shop. As he was cutting my hair, he kept up the usual line of chatter. "Can't wait for the new season. Every Sunday I sit down in my living room, turn on the tube and watch you run around. I can always tell who you are. You're running all around, you're in charge of the game and you know what you're doing. It's going to be great watching good old Number Thirty-seven working again."

My number is 56. Number 37 is Burl Toler. He's black. No wonder my ears always get nicked. At least by Harry.

Poise is another ingredient in refereeing. That's so necessary. The ability to remain calm when all hell is breaking loose—that's poise. Players are emotional, coaches are too involved, so the referee has to be calm and poised.

You have to have a belief in yourself. Confidence is the name of the game. You must feel that you're right on top of everything. Nothing can happen that can stump you. At least that's the feeling you have to have. Nothing gives confidence as much as preparation. You must prepare thoroughly. Nothing is left to chance. Solid experience is one of the big items in preparation. Physical conditioning is part of preparation. A referee doesn't have any substitutes during a game. If he gets hurt, the crew adjusts and works with one fewer official. I ride my stationary bicycle seven miles every day, walk two miles and do stomach exercises every morning.

Guts. You got to have it. A football referee is in the rejection business. Every time he makes a decision, 50 percent of the people involved thinks he's wrong. You can't please everyone. Don't try. Just please yourself. And Commissioner Rozelle. But you had better be right. Make the tough call. Don't worry about the reaction. It's necessary to have that mental toughness. Toughness plus hard work equals success. A NFL referee does what every other referee throughout the country does, only he has to do it better and more often.

Communications. It's more than talk. Your nonverbal actions on the field are much more significant than your verbal comments. How you walk, how you keep your head on your shoulders and how you create an impression are so very decisive for success.

Whenever I hear someone say "give him the finger," I think of Pete Gogolak, the Hungarian field goal kicker of the New York

Giants. Not the way you think though. This is all open and above-board. It happened from a lack of nonverbal communication. Or verbal communication without words. Sign language maybe.

I was in New York for a game a couple of seasons ago. The Giants had just scored their first touchdown. Pete Gogolak trotted in for the extra-point try. I asked Gogolak, "Where do you want the ball placed? Two- or three-yard line?"

Gogolak ran by me, turned and had two fingers of his hand stuck out, above his thumb which was also extended. I placed the ball on the three-yard line. He made the extra-point try. As he ran off the field, he stopped for a second and told me, "I wanted the ball placed on the two-yard line."

I answered, "Wait a minute, Gogolak. You put out three fingers to me." I illustrated what he had done—top two fingers straight out, with the thumb extended out below the two fingers.

"That's only two where I come from. We don't ever count the thumb."

I've been lucky. Though it's a life of pressures and much rejection, it's one that I would never change. My calls are like bottles that are marked "no deposit, no return." You have to enjoy it. You have to remember that it is high-level competition, where talent is almost equal. But that little extra edge (shove, push or any foul) can be the difference. That's the job.

Every week it's a different city. I never know if I'm coming or going. That's the one thing players and coaches agree on. One Sunday it's Washington, D.C., the following week it's San Francisco, then New York, then Miami, then Detroit, San Diego, Foxboro, Oakland and New Orleans. It could be any one of 26 cities. And after a while, they all look alike. There is an airport, a hotel room, several meetings, film reviews, the ball game, and then run to catch a plane back home to Los Angeles. Some cities are easier to get into than others. More important though, some cities are easier to get out of than others. And that's what counts.

It's well over 125,000 miles a season for me. Since I started to referee in this league, I have flown over two and a half million miles. Sometimes I meet myself returning to the West Coast when I'm going to the East Coast. Too often I just know where I am going. And not know the name of both teams. I'm sure of the home team, but sometimes I forget who the visiting team is.

I was in Washington, D.C., one weekend. I checked into the hotel, and later got into the elevator to go to dinner. On the fourth floor, Charley Winner, coach of the St. Louis Cardinals then, got on the same elevator. He said, "Hi, Norm. How are you?"

"Fine, Coach. What are you doing in Washington?"

Coach Winner stared at me. "We're playing here tomorrow."

The elevator stopped, I got off and Winner watched me walk away. A strange look was on his face. You know, one of those "Gosh, it's going to be another long afternoon tomorrow. The referee doesn't even know who's playing."

Come to think of it, it was a long afternoon that next day.

It happened in Minneapolis one cold fall day. The game was heating up, and I was glad it was half time. Maybe a cup of hot coffee would warm me up. Joe Connell and I started to run for the officials' dressing room just as the gun sounded, ending the first half. We ran toward the exit at the end of the field. As I was about to walk through the door, some fan in the stands was waving his program and shouting at the top of his voice.

"Hey, Norm. How are you? How's the family—the wife and boys? Can I come down to see you after the game? Lots to tell you."

I looked at him. He didn't look familiar, but he sounded familiar. I yelled back, "Sure, come on down to the dressing room after the game." I waved and started through the door. I turned to Connell and asked, "Joe, what city are we in?"

Connell said, "Minneapolis."

I knew then it must be my former neighbor who had moved back there five years ago. It's getting so you can't tell a fan without a program. Especially if you don't know where you are!

The Biggest Game

Super Bowl One was the game that brought the two rival leagues, the AFL and the NFL, together. It made professional football into one large organization. In fact, it was the showdown, as it was the first meeting of the two merged leagues. There were six officials to work that game, along with six alternates. That made 12 officials in uniform. It was the first and only time in professional football that there were more officials than players from one team on the field. Only six of us had authority to make calls though.

One hour prior to kickoff, I met the two teams' captains at the center of the field. Green Bay called the toss as the visiting team that day. Willie Davis, captain of the Packers, yelled "Heads!" Green Bay always yelled "Heads!" Coach Vince Lombardi had a theory that the eagle side of the silver dollar weighed more.

Heads it was. Davis chose to receive. As the captains turned to walk away, Jerry Mays, captain of the Kansas City Chiefs, came back and asked, "Hey, Ref. Can I have the coin as a souvenir?"

I shook my head. "No way," I answered, "you lost the toss."

A silver dollar is tough to find, especially a lucky one. It had to be lucky, for I needed all the help in the world when I worked.

When the Green Bay Packers won the toss in Super Bowl One, that gave them the choice of two options. They could either take the ball, which was to receive the kickoff, or defend either goal. One or the other. Most teams always take the ball, unless it is a very windy day. They then might want to kick off, and have the wind at their back. This game, though, was played in Los Angeles, so that really meant no choice. The winner of the coin toss would elect to receive the ball.

Willie Davis, one of the two captains of Green Bay and as smart as they come, said, "Norm, we would like to receive at that end." He pointed to the end he meant.

I looked at Willie and couldn't keep from smiling. He wanted both choices. He had done that to me before. And fooled me once. Not today though. He would have slickered Jerry Mays to say, "Okay, then we'll defend the other goal." Before Mays could say anything, I spoke up and told Willie, "I should think you would like that. But you don't have both options. Pick one or the other."

It had almost worked. Mays and Lenny Dawson, the other captain of the Chiefs who was out there, laughed. It wouldn't have been funny if I had let Willie get away with it. The Chiefs would have blamed me for losing the game. You know, like starting at a disadvantage. You blame anyone you can when you lose.

Davis walked away, talking to me over his shoulder. "You should have let it go. It was none of your business."

It was my business. Davis was thinking Green Bay all the time. My job is to think both teams all the time.

Super Bowl One had a split crew of officials—three from the NFL and three from AFL. I was the referee. In the second quarter Bart Starr, the Packers' great quarterback, threw a pass to Carroll Dale in the end zone. The head linesman, one of the three NFL officials, had his flag down for illegal motion. When I nullified the play and took the touchdown away, I explained why to Bart Starr and Bob Skoronski, the offensive captains of the Packers. They both looked at each other. Bart Starr finally turned to me and asked, "Who threw the flag?"

I pointed to the head linesman. Starr then asked, "Why did he throw his flag? Isn't he one of our guys?"

There are no "our guys" when you work a game. Officials don't choose up sides. They catch hell from both sides.

The Kansas City Chiefs had a fine team. Well coached, well disciplined, but a bit awed by the Packers' reputation. They looked scared. Not physically, but of the Packers' reputation. From the coin toss before the game, I had a feeling that the Chiefs felt as if they couldn't win. The pre-game publicity for the Packers, the established reputation of the NFL, and the tremendous coverage by television, radio and the press seemed to inhibit the Chiefs. Another day at another place under regular game conditions might have changed the outcome. Not that day though. It was just a matter of time for the Packers to pull away and put the game away. And they did.

That was the game with "The Hammer." Remember Fred Williamson, cornerback of the Chiefs? Williamson's hammer tackle would come as a cocked right hand which stunned the runner when it was applied. He brought the hand across the runner's head. Very effective too. It was a tough hit. The reporters kept writing how The Hammer was going to wipe out Jim Taylor, Paul Hornung and the other Packer runners.

Before the game several of the Packers laughingly told me, "Watch out for The Hammer. Don't let him get you." It was a running routine with them. I don't know if it was for real or not. All I know is that in the fourth quarter, Donny Anderson, the big bonus player for the Packers, ran the ball. Gale Gillingham, one of the offensive guards of the Packers, was leading the interference. He was Fuzzy Thurston's substitute, and he was really moving. I followed the play and Gillingham's knee hit Williamson, The Hammer, in the head as he tried to wipe out the blocker. Down went The Hammer. They had to carry Williamson off the field. As they were carrying The Hammer on a stretcher, Jim Taylor turned toward me and said, "There goes The Hammer. It was supposed to be me." He laughed.

Let me tell you about Roger. Here's a typical day for him. Change the script but the ending is always the same. Roger is a neighbor of mine. He rolled out of bed late one morning. His alarm didn't go off. His daughter was in the bathroom, fixing her hair. She wouldn't get out until she was through. By this time Roger was fit to be tied, but couldn't say anything as he was rushing to make up some lost time. When he cut himself shaving, his son made some smart-alecky remark. He backed his car out of the garage and picked up a nail and his tire went flat. He ran for the bus, paid his fare and was elbowed back to the rear. Some fat, sharp-tongued lady kept jawing at him all the way to work. When he sat down at his desk for a breather, the office manager chewed him out for not getting some reports done.

It was one of those days. Everyone had something to tell him.

Fortunately, his son had his tire repaired and left his car in the parking lot. Now he didn't have to fight the bus crowd home. On the way home he barely made a signal, but the policeman didn't think so. Not only did he get a ticket for going through the red light, he also received a long lecture on the dangers of driving. He sat still and had to listen.

When he arrived home, there wasn't a beer in the house. His wife told him that she wouldn't stock it anymore. It wasn't good for him. Said he was too fat. The dinner was burned, and he received lots more badgering from his family. When the dinner was finally over, and his wife quiet for a moment, he grabbed his hat and made a break for the door.

His wife saw him leaving and shouted, "Roger, where do you think you're going?"

Roger didn't even look back as he hollered, "I'm going to the football game and give that referee hell."

The stands are full of Rogers. That's why I keep the sign Roger over my desk.

Don't get me wrong. I had one helluva ride those 22 years. And I enjoyed every minute of it. Every minute of every game that I refereed has been a lasting memory to me. No matter how much fun you think it is out on the field, it's at least 500 percent more fun than you can ever imagine. I've been one of the lucky ones. I've walked those white lines, blown the whistle and pulled off the striped shirt. It's been great. And laugh—I thought I'd die. Come to think of it, I almost did many times. But what a way to go.

Sudden Death

Super Bowl X was over. Done. The game went smoothly without a hitch. An occasional bitch, but no problems. The reporters around the country were kind for a change. Even the ones who had ripped us pretty good over the years. It never had bothered me. But I would be lying in my teeth if I said that I didn't enjoy going out with those sweet-tasting comments. Doug Krikorian, of the Los Angeles *Herald-Examiner*, wrote, "The officiating was excellent with instant replays proving their judgment sound on all close plays. It's unfortunate this group headed by Norm Schachter can't work all NFL games." Larry Guest, of the *Orlando Sentinel Star*, wrote, "Even the zebras were super. With officiating controversy dotted throughout the past season, it seemed only fitting that a monumental blunder by the striped shirts should decide the Super Bowl. But never before have so many close calls been ratified by the telling evidence of the slow-motion cameras. Never before has a crew of officials maintained such complete control of an emotional hard-hitting game, even though only two penalties were called."

When reporters start saying nice things like that, it's time to pack it in. Quit when you're ahead. I did. Like I said before, I'd rather be lucky than good. And you're only as good as your last call.

It's tough to walk off the field. It's tougher to walk away from 22 years of bang-bang excitement. There's no sense washing all that controversial experience down the drain. So I work for the

218

League office. I look for new officials, and evaluate the officials every Sunday at some pro game. I also do a lot of speaking to groups along the circuit. I still co-edit the rule book, make up the yearly rules review exam for all the officials, and I write the weekly quiz review lessons for the various crews' conferences.

Do I miss it? Sure, I miss it. I miss the camaraderie, the on-the-field excitement and being a part of it. But I was there 22 exciting years, and I enjoy sharing it with others now.

Truisms of a Professional Football Referee

---

1. It's comforting to know you have a mother and father when the coaches tell you differently.

2. Always count on a poor picture in instant replay—for you.

3. If the fans and players don't know who worked the ball game, you've had a great game.

4. The day you stop enjoying the game, get the hell away from the field.

5. You're only as good as your last call.

6. Sometimes it's better to be lucky than good—but not in the long run.

7. Always remember that the only friends you have during a football game are the other officials—and keep an eye on them.

8. You have to be perfect the first game, and then get better in every game the following weeks.

9. When a coach says, "I don't want any breaks. Just give me my fair advantage," he really means, "Give us all the close ones."

10. Don't waste time second-guessing yourself, for there will be millions who will do it for you.

11. It's a sure bet that a coach's friendliness before the game is blown away with the opening whistle.

12. Whenever you have a tight plane connection after the game, there will be enough rhubarbs during the game to make you miss the plane.

13. If you're lucky, you'll outlast every coach in the League.

14. A former ballplayer turned TV commentator remembers all the "bum calls" you made against him.

15. Any referee who hasn't made a mistake hasn't worked too many games.

16. The only time to worry about a bad ball game is when only your dog is happy to see you when you come home.

17. When a player loses it in his legs, he gains it in his mouth.

18. The only thing a referee really has to know is whether it's right or wrong.

19. Don't worry about a coach's antics on the sidelines, for every coach is hired to be fired.

20. Referees are like people—some good and some not so good.